Classroom Skills
A Teachers' Guide

Jean Hull

David Fulton Publishers
London

David Fulton Publishers Ltd
2 Barbon Close, London WC1N 3JX

First published in Great Britain by
David Fulton Publishers, 1990

Note: The right of Jean Hull to be identified as the author of this work has been
asserted by her in accordance with the Copyright, Designs and Patents Act 1988.

© Jean Hull

British Library Cataloguing in Publication Data

Hull, Jean
  Classroom skills : a teachers' guide.
  1. Schools. Teaching
  I. Title
  371.102

  ISBN 1-85346-131-8

Cartoons by Ellis James-Robertson (Bob)
Design by Almac Ltd
Typeset by Chapterhouse, Formby
Printed in Great Britain by BPCC Wheatons Ltd, Exeter

Contents

Introduction 1

1 On Entering a School 5

2 Are You Sitting Comfortably? Then I'll Begin 21

3 First Catch Your Pupil 35

4 Exploding the Myth of the Normal Child 51

5 'You Gotta Accentuate the Positive' 75

6 Keeping Tabs 91

7 The Feedback Loop 109

8 Life Support Systems 119

On a Personal Note 131

Glossary of Educational Acronyms 132

Further Reading 133

Index 135

'Education is political.'

Introduction

'English education: Oh! it lacks coordination' *Noel Coward*

Who is this book for?

It is intended to help all types of teachers-in-training, inexperienced teachers, probationers and those about to enter teaching to become 'professional' in the best sense of the word without too many tears. It will *not* tell you what to teach, nor how to teach specific subjects. It is presumed that you have acquired such knowledge elsewhere in your training.

It is also designed for course tutors and for those teachers in schools who have responsibility for staff development. It is written with an awareness of the essentially different climate and demands that are now placed on all phases of education. My own experience as a tutor in education and schools' inspector has shown, and is supported by the evidence of others, (Montgomery and Hadfield, 1989), that on many initial teacher education courses there is unsufficient pedagogical training. Also a recent survey (Swanwick and Chitty, 1989) gives depressing evidence of poor support for PGCE students on teaching practice from teacher supervisors in schools. Few gave minimal support on such vital matters as class management or lesson planning, citing as reasons lack of time, training and resources.

In the sixties the view of many in teacher training was that it was more important 'to produce well educated people than to produce technically competent practitioners' (Jeffreys, 1961). The popular view today is that that policy was an unmitigated disaster, producing neither! A bit extreme maybe, but I have to confess to some sympathy with the Prince of Wales when I recall the number of times I have winced at spelling mistakes and the poor grammar presented to pupils by teachers.

Pedagogy is not *what* to teach, but the nitty gritty of *how* to. For it is not the slightest use to be brimful of knowledge and skill which you are bursting to pass on and share with a younger generation without the cooperation of your pupils. If you cannot create a good learning environment, which means an orderly classroom – the sort of atmosphere which is conducive to joyful learning, and you have – and use – the appropriate range of skills to communicate your knowledge, then you fail as a teacher. To be an enthusiastic amateur is not good enough. What must be added to this enthusiasm are the professional skills that every good teacher demonstrates, often so effortlessly that after a time they are not conscious of them. However, those very teachers are often allocated to students on teaching practice, but because they may never have been required to analyse those abilities which make them so successful they may not find it easy to pass on their skills. To them this book is also dedicated, in the hope that it may ease their increasingly difficult roles.

The mark of a top professional in any sphere is to make it seem effortless. Think of watching the public performances of your favourite first class artists – be they dancers, singers, skaters, sportsmen, or instrumentalists. It all looks so easy! Yet we know that behind each skilled performance is meticulous preparation and the long slog of practice. The same is true of teaching. *Do not* expect it to be easy from the start: or that you will get it right first go. *Do* expect to have to put in a lot of preparation and practise: to appraise and adjust your performance until you get it right. *Do* expect to succeed, and to continue improving your performance.

What is this book about?

It is about the 'how to' of teaching. The many changes in education over recent years mean fundamental changes in both attitude and practice in all aspects of the teaching profession.

First, teacher education and training is moving towards a range of possible modes of entry into the profession via BEd, PGCE, licensed, and articled teachers. The pattern of training to become an efficient teacher may vary widely, and in some cases has yet to be determined. The picture is further clouded by the trend to amalgamate colleges of higher education with universities, whilst both are still coming to terms with the CATE 1984 criteria for teacher education courses.

Secondly, the Education Reform Act 1988 has fundamentally changed our education system. The introduction of the National

Curriculum with its requirements for assessment and testing at key stages and GCSE, BTEC, TVEI, and the many other new examinations and qualifications such as profiles of achievement, will mean radical changes to the traditional ways of imparting knowledge and assessing its assimilation.

Thirdly, the practice of teacher appraisal is steadily gaining ground in line with commerce and industry.

The educational field is now vastly different for new recruits to the teaching profession. Although there are many untried fields for you to explore and develop, the need, then as now, for a teaching force with good pedagogical skills is paramount. This means on the one hand understanding how children and young people learn, acquire skills and knowledge, and on the other how to create an environment in which to impart those skills and knowledge. This must not be seen simply as a rag-bag of pragmatic ideas, but linked firmly to a clear understanding of the underlying concepts of teaching which will then unify your practice.

This book aims to help you to acquire some of that expertise. *It is a guide to action not a recipe for success.*

Chapter 1 should help you with your initial visits to schools (perhaps for the first time since you left school yourself). It deals with protocol as a visitor and on teaching practice, and the skills of observation and study. Chapters 2 and 3 deal with actual delivery of your lessons; Chapters 4 and 5 with deviations from the 'norm', that is learning and behavioural difficulties. Chapters 6 and 7 are concerned with evaluation of pupils and yourself. Chapter 8 is on what you should expect to be available once you are in post.

Chapters 3 to 6 end with a summary for quick and easy reference. There is an educational glossary for the many acronyms you are expected to know, and a further reading list for those who wish to read in more depth on particular aspects of teaching.

Good teaching is never a soft option. It never was, and children will ensure that it never is. But it can be one of the most rewarding experiences life has to offer.

Good teaching!

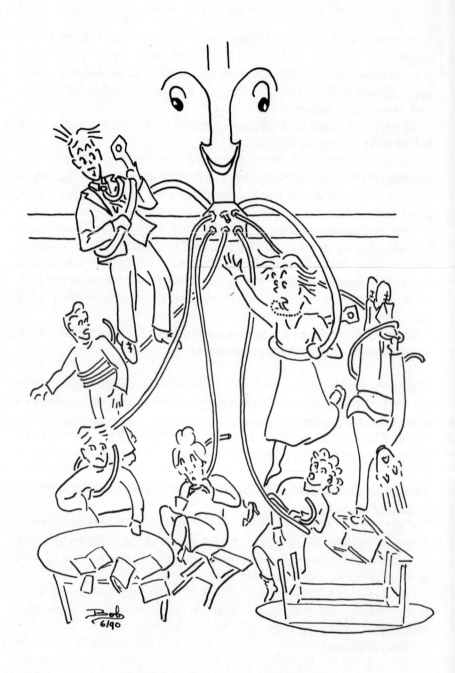

'A school is a living dynamic organism.'

CHAPTER 1

On entering a school

What are schools for?

Doubtless you will have asked – and been asked – this question in sessions on the history and philosophy of education. All schools are now required to produce a handbook or brochure in which their reasons for existing, their 'aims', are made explicit. Phrases such as 'fostering the development of the individual' are common, and there is often a statement on cultural values and the maintenance of high academic and behavioural standards. In other words there is a commitment to educate the pupils in the cultural, academic and moral traditions of this country.

Less explicit, but nonetheless powerful, reasons for their existence are:

Statute

Parents are obliged by law to send their children over the age of five to a school; and state schools are obliged to accept them and aprovide them with an education 'appropriate to their age and ability'.

Investment

This country needs, as never before, a highly trained workforce if it is to gain its position in world trade markets, or indeed maintain its present high standard of living.

Social

There are still a large number of poor families in this country; poor in both material and cultural terms. Most schools regard it as part of their responsibility to compensate in some way for this deprivation.

More recently many schools have expanded their roles into their local communities, providing not just opportunities for adult education, but experimenting with new ways of working with their local groups, businesses and industries in an effort to break away from the popular view of their isolated existence.

Yet another significant expansion of the school's role is in the radical notion of training teachers on-the-job. There are schemes for graduates to enter teaching directly and complete a PGCE part-time over two years to become articled teachers, and for suitably educated mature people to start teaching right away as licensed teachers, but follow a two year part-time course. The implications for schools here are profound, for not only will schools' remit be to teach their pupils but some of their teachers as well. This calls for a considerable expansion of the teacher-tutor schemes that exist in a number of authorities. The Inner London Education Authority (ILEA), for instance, ran such a scheme, whereby experienced senior teachers were allocated responsibility (and time) to act as tutors to students on teaching practice and to probationary teachers. To meet this need Hargreaves has proposed the setting up of training schools or consortia. A further innovative training course was one operated jointly by Lewisham schools and Avery Hill College as a one year part-time course for teachers in primary, secondary and special schools to tackle the issues of continuity and progression at transfer age. Lecturers, Inspectors and teachers joint-taught the course to great effect.

A school is a living dynamic organism; any living organism which does not grow dies. It is that simple. Expect to be part of a changing institution.

What makes a good school?

The *Primary School Project* published by ILEA in 1986, sought to tease out the answer to this question, and came up with a list of twelve factors which were to be found in effective primary schools. Check them, if you like, against a school you know well.

(1) Purposeful leadership of the staff by the headteacher.
(2) The involvement of the deputy headteacher.

(3) The involvement of teachers in planning and developing initiatives.
(4) Consistency amongst teachers, in approach and agreed policies.
(5) Structured sessions, in other words an organised framework within which pupils can work, yet be allowed some freedom within the structure.
(6) Intellectually challenging teaching, where pupils will expect, and be expected, to achieve good results.
(7) Work centred environment, with a high level of pupil industry and only work related movement in class.
(8) Limited focus within sessions, that is to say one curriculum area at a time, rather than mixed activities.
(9) Maximum communication between teachers and pupils.
(10) Record keeping.
(11) Parental involvement.
(12) Positive climate, where there is a greater emphasis on praise and reward than on punishment and critical control.

Do not be too discouraged if the school you find yourself in for teaching practice falls short on these virtues. We don't live in a perfect world, even in education, but such schools do exist, and in increasing numbers.

What makes a good teacher?

A very useful exercise to try when you first start your teacher training is to note down your recollections of your own schooling. How many schools did you attend? How different were they, and in what respects – strict/easy going, large/small? Were they enjoyable? Presumably they were as you now want to teach. Try to analyse what it was that made them enjoyable; what aspects of the school you best remember, and which you remember with displeasure, fear, or even hate. Be honest; it is a private exercise! Think of the teacher(s) you most admired and learned from; perhaps they inspired you to take a certain direction in life. Describe their attributes, especially those which you think made them successful teachers. Now think of the worst teacher(s) you encountered. Why were they so bad or hated? List their attributes, especially those which you think contributed to their poor performance or status. Keep these notes and 'ponder them in your heart' from time to time. You will find them a reassurance, especially during teaching practice!

Several studies (Docking, 1980, Hargreaves, 1972, and others) have attempted to identify the features of a good teacher by consumer research amongst pupils, and the sort of portrait that emerges has the following elements:

Personality

Makes the day a pleasant one with a few jokes; treats you as a person and knows your name; takes your ideas seriously and isn't arrogant; listens, and tries to understand; is tactful, does not impose formality for the sake of preserving discipline; is cheerful, humorous, and doesn't take himself too seriously; accepts people's weaknesses; provides standards and offers a good example; encourages you to make your own choices and decisions; doesn't wear outlandish clothes.

Discipline

Keeps order, is firm but not overbearing; doesn't get upset, disturbed or angry as a result of misbehaviour; is strict, but nevertheless enables you to learn; is fair, has no favourites, punishes justly.

Teaching

Organises the class so that pupils feel work is being done; gives guidance on what is 'good' work; gives clear explanations and helps you to understand; helps you to learn and feel confident; teaches in an interesting way; puts something of interest in the lesson and shows that the activities have a rationale; teaches.

Pupils do *not* like (and therefore neither respect nor learn from) a teacher who is too easy going or too strict; punishes unfairly or excessively; has 'favourites' or 'picks on' pupils; doesn't help or explain; is dull, boring and doesn't know his subject well; ignores individual differences (eg punishing a whole class for the misdemeanours of a few immediately alienates the law-abiding who are understandably outraged); ridicules and is sarcastic. Other pungent comments noted from pupils are 'Does he think we're stupid?' 'We're not being asked to think', and so on. In time no doubt you will collect your own store of such piercing home truths.

Looked at another way this daunting list of paragon virtues can provide the framework for professional training as 'what-is-to-be-aimed-for'.

> Inspections of secondary schools have shown that good secondary teachers have command of their subject, and are enthusiastic about teaching it, and perceive the contribution it can make to the whole curriculum. They use a range of resources and are not reliant on the use of worksheets and the copying of notes. (HMI (1987) *Quality in Schools*, Department of Education and Science.)

The same survey states that

> Effective teachers help pupils develop lively, enquiring minds; acquire understanding, knowledge, and skills; develop personal moral values; and appreciate human endeavour and aspirations. They have a sensitive understanding of the society in which their pupils are growing up, its racial and cultural mix, and the pace and effect of technological change. They are able to establish a quiet but purposeful working atmosphere, to organise the teaching and learning so that the work matches the different aptitudes and abilities of the children, and to relate and adapt their methods to the needs and circumstances of the moment. This entails setting high expectations, with pupils extended to their full capacity. To this end, the teachers employ class, group, and individual teaching to suit the kinds of learning demanded. The best teachers are well informed about individual pupils and are discerning in the identification of their needs. They use a variety of techniques to encourage and assess progress, including careful and informed observation, perceptive and constructive comment, and a variety of formal measures. With such teachers the children attain high standards of work and are encouraged to live and work amicably together, to show consideration for others and to have respect for their environment.
>
> These characteristics are common in some measure to all good teachers and are constant and fundamental.

I make no apology for the length of the above quotation, for there is none better. It summarises the attributes and answers the question posed at the beginning of this section 'What makes a good teacher?' It is not just a counsel of perfection; an ideal that may be unattainable. It is culled from concrete evidence of real teachers at the chalk face.

Professional studies

A 1989 DES circular states that qualified teacher status will not be awarded unless there is evidence of a satisfactory standard of practical classroom work, including the ability to ensure that effective teaching and learning can take place and to manage pupil behaviour. In addition to saying that primary school teachers will not be able to opt out of training to teach religious education, and must spend one hundred hours of their course on science (in line with English and maths), the circular lays down new criteria for teacher education.

> The new criteria reflect the importance of the national curriculum and the need for newly-trained teachers to be able to contribute to its delivery on entering employment.
>
> Institutions should ensure that experienced teachers from schools are involved in:
>
> ● the planning of initial teaching training courses and in their evaluation;
> ● the selection of students; and
> ● the supervision and assessment of students' practical work...
>
> Courses should prepare students for teaching the full range of pupils and for the diversity of ability, behaviour, social background and ethnic and cultural origin they are likely to encounter among pupils in ordinary schools.
>
> There should be practical classroom experience during the first term of a course. All courses should include a sustained period of teaching practice... and other school experience in more than one school (75 to 100 days).

The HMI survey on teacher education, *Quality in Schools*, published by the DES in 1987 states:

> The qualities which are fundamental to good teaching will not change, whatever new demands are placed upon teachers and the taught. Nevertheless, these demands will continue, as new ideas emerge and new policies evolve. They include those from government; from the criteria for GCSE; from the introduction of CPVE and TVEI; from specific grant related in-service initiatives; and from the social, economic and technological changes affecting society at large, employment, and education and training.

To that formidable list must now be added the many implications of the Education Reform Act 1988, with its mandatory national curriculum and allied assessment and testing requirements.

Do not despair! Remember that initial teacher training is just that; an initial introduction to the complex skills of your chosen profession. You will need to continue to study and attend courses on a continuing basis throughout your career.

You may also have views on developing your inimitable teaching 'style'. Again, do not worry. This is something that will develop in time, given the secure framework that good organisation and preparation provides, and the freedom to be creative, which is the essence of job satisfaction in teaching.

Students' views on a professional studies course

It may be of interest to include some of the comments made by students on the evaluation of their secondary professional studies course.

On giving presentations in small group seminars – '...gives us confidence and practice for the real thing.'

'Beginning the course with reflections on our own school days was very beneficial.'

'Preparation for attachment (extended visits) was essential and appreciated by all, and although the time element was short a lot was learned through the experience.'

'Discussion within the group (on visits and TP experiences) was valuable and encouraging.'

'Aims and objectives were done very thoroughly. This has now given me much clearer ideas for planning my lessons.'

'Visiting infant, junior and special schools – because we are all involved in education, and teachers must be prepared to look at what has gone before, or what is to come in order to gain the insight to make an appropriate contribution at whatever level they may find themselves working.'

'...where the emphasis on teacher training should lie – how to do the job and putting the polish on common sense. I have been made to think and act in situations in which I will find myself in school.'

'The informal "safe house" policy helps build up oral fluency, confidence and practice in public expression and coherent communication to others.'

'Making the students work quickly and to time limits was very useful, particularly as their future employment will impose these.'

'I have found the course interesting and useful. I wonder how I would have coped on teaching practice without this information.'

'It is good to see the tutors putting into practice the methods and strategies they teach!'

School visiting

Very early on in your course you should be given the opportunity to visit a range of schools. To the uninitiated this is always a bewildering experience. If, therefore, you are to gain the maximum benefit from these changes, it is essential that you prepare yourself fully.

Obviously you will want to make notes on what you see. The trouble at first is to recognise precisely what it is that you are seeing. In order to put your observations and experiences into context it is helpful to prepare your notebook beforehand under the following headings or groupings. Some of this information should already be available to you so that you do not waste your own and other people's time in asking during the visit.

Note down:

(1) The name and type of school (Infant, JMI, Middle, Secondary, etc).
(2) The name of the Headteacher and the teacher in charge of your visit.
(3) The number and age range of the pupils.
(4) The catchment area.
(5) The number of teachers.
(6) The number and arrangement of the classes (vertical groupings, mixed ability, streamed, etc).

Classroom observation techniques

Depending on whether your visit is a brief half day one, or a more extended attachment of several days, the extent and depth of observation will vary. If you can, focus on one of the following areas at a time so that you do not become totally confused.

(1) Class arrangements and organisation.
(2) Teacher–pupil interactions, (how much? when? amount of active learning?).
(3) The teacher: arrival and dismissal procedures; style; presentation; pace; variety; levels of work; questioning.
(4) The children: time spent silent (listening, working); doing, talking to each other, to teacher; questioning; sitting; moving about; how many never get involved; who are the leaders/ followers?
(5) School organisation: times; movement procedures; meals; punishments; staff duties.

(6) Subject organisation: equipment storage, organisation, distribution and collection.

This list may seem formidable, and if your visit is a brief one you will not have the chance to cover more than a fraction of it. If you are on your own, decide what you want to concentrate on and stick to those areas. If, however, you are in a small group, it is more useful to divide the list out between you so that later you can present a composite picture to each other.

If your visit extends over more than a day, ask if it can be arranged for you to accompany one pupil for a half or a full day. Look at their timetable and see what the rest of the week consists of: how many moves they have to make; the range and sequence of subjects they study. This is particularly revealing at secondary level, especially in the first year. It is an exercise that few teachers can do, but it can be valuable for it often shows the stresses that a school system places new, young children under. For instance, in one school I found that the first year pupils had twenty-two different teachers in a week, and were expected to know the idiosyncracies of all twenty-two and what their subjects required of the pupils.

Is it surprising how often performance and attainment, and indeed behaviour, regress in that first year? For instance, is the teacher of French aware that the class has just come in from an exhilarating games lesson, or, conversely, a lesson where no talking or movement at all was allowed? This system of Pavlovian conditioning whereby humans are expected to respond to a bell at 40 minute intervals by instant physical and mental switches of activity must be unique to education, for there is no job that makes the same bizarre and stressful demands on its workers. When one remembers that these same children have recently come from a primary school regime where they are usually taught for most of the time by one teacher in one classroom, the change to the demands of the average secondary school are, for many, quite terrifying, and for a very few, too much to cope with altogether. More schools are now recognising this and make sensitive arrangements for transfer.

Teaching practice

Teaching practice is often viewed with mixed feelings by both students and tutors alike. It is a paradoxical situation, on the one hand offering the first opportunity to be delivering rather than receiving education, bringing together theory and practice, and, on the other hand your position in the class may seem to both you and the pupils somewhat uncertain and ambiguous for you are at one and the same time both pupil and teacher.

'Sitting next to Nellie'

The oldest form of industrial training is based on the principle of apprenticeship. That is, working directly under the eye of a highly skilled worker, and observing and absorbing the particular skills of the job. Recently it has fallen into disrepute in industry as being inefficient, but that may be due more to the lack of skilled 'Nellies' than to the system itself. However, the accepted mode of entry to teaching in the early part of this century was via 'pupil teachers'; well educated school leavers who assisted the class teacher for a year or so before going on to teacher training. This is within the memory of some retired teachers who feel it had much to recommend it. Certainly the new proposals for teacher training would indicate some recognition of this. The main ingredient for success of any such scheme must be that 'Nellie' herself is properly trained for this new role. Nevertheless the best advice for you on teaching practice is to find a good 'Nellie' and observe and analyse the elements of their successful teaching. In turn, a good 'Nellie' will be able to offer you that essential part of training – instant and constructive feedback on your own performance, so that you can modify it in time for the next session, and not have to wait for a visit from your college tutor.

Teaching practice is an experience that, in general, is highly valued by students, but the outcomes and effects are totally unpredictable.

Schools and etiquette

So that you can concentrate on the job in hand – teaching the lessons you have so carefully prepared – it is sensible to get to know 'your' school and its idiosyncracies as soon as possible. Once they are known, you are less likely to fall foul of its rules, thereby adding to the already considerable pressures of teaching practice itself. The main source of this sort of information is likely to be the teacher tutor. There will be one teacher in the school whose responsibility is for students. S/he should give you clear information (preferably written) on such matters as:

(1) *School times, meals, and breaks*

(2) *Management structures* The names and roles of the senior members of staff and heads of departments, and the 'chains of command'. Even if you are not necessarily going to be meeting them it is wise to know who you may be talking to and to whom you should refer for help in curriculum or pastoral matters. They may be different, especially in large secondary schools.

(3) *Rules* Good schools have few, and those mostly positive, but be sure you are aware of them.

(4) *Safety and incident reporting procedures* That is, what to do in case of fire or other emergencies, as well as general safety precautions in the school and your classroom. And what procedures to take and who to report to in case of any accident or other untoward incident while you are in charge of a group of children. If you are likely to be accompanying children outside the school, on an educational visit, swimming or a games match, for instance, then although you will not be in sole charge, you must be quite clear on the accepted procedures.

(5) *Codes of practice* For marking work and keeping records. For discipline; to whom should you report serious matters of indiscipline or abuse, either to you or to other pupils? You need to be reassured that there is a secure backup system to help you when the occasion warrants it.

(6) *Equipment* Equipment covers everything from footballs and gym mats to computers, overhead projectors, tape recorders, musical instruments, and even the ancient Banda or any other reprographic machine the school may possess. Make sure you know where all the equipment is kept that you are likely to want to use, and the procedures governing its use. (Do you sign for it? Ask a technician? Have to give notice in advance?) Who will show you how to use it properly, and to whom do you report damage, breakage or loss?

(7) *School calendar* What major events are scheduled during the time you will be in the school, for example sports days, parents' evenings, plays or concerts?

(8) *Registers* This is the one document that schools are legally required to maintain. Probably you will not be required to fill them in on teaching practice, but make sure you see how it is done.

Staff handbook

Many good schools compile a staff handbook which contains all this sort of information. Its purpose is to ensure that all staff are cognisant of the systems and procedures that operate within the school. This is not nearly so bureaucratic as it might at first seem. In small schools in particular it is frequently assumed that *because* they are small, and everyone knows everyone else, channels of communication are good, everyone knows what is the 'rule', and what is going on. Unfortunately this is seldom true, and even the smallest school benefits from a brief outline on such matters. The staff handbook is of greatest value, of course, for supply, part-time, new or probationary teachers, and is obviously welcomed by students on teaching practice. There is no harm in asking if the school has one!

Personal appearances

This is a subject known to raise more emotional 'heat' than most. In the past what was or was not acceptable attire was fairly clear. Collars and ties for men, and skirts of a 'decent' length for women. Today, fashions not only change quickly, but there is a very wide range of styles which are considered 'fashionable', so it is more difficult to indicate with any certainty what should or should not be worn by teachers. Indeed there are some who will declare it presumptuous should anyone dare to make any comment on appearance at all! Nevertheless certain facts have to be faced.

More than almost any other job (except actors, with whom they have a lot in common) teachers are on public display for the whole of their working time. Whether you like it or not, you are a 'performer' giving a 'performance' for your pupils, and many of the skills of the actor must be yours.

Many jobs carry either a uniform, or require clothing that is suitable for the task in hand. In this way do we recognise those with official roles like police, fire, or postmen or women. Or the job itself dictates what is worn, like safety helmets and boots for miners and those in the construction industries. Presumably you would not wear the same clothes to a disco, to hillclimb, or paint a wall. So clothes should be suitable for the job. The fashion for very short mini-skirts gave rise to numerous, mostly unprintable, stories of young teachers and the antics of adolescent boys. 'Don't expose yourself to ridicule' was the best advice in those circumstances!

An argument commonly offered to counter any suggestions of constraint on personal choice in such matters is the one 'I'm me, and it's my intellect that is being trained and used. What I wear isn't important.' I'm afraid it is! And for the following reasons.

Clothes are the first thing we notice about people. Think of the snap judgments we make of people based on a split second's glance. It may be that later we are surprised and wrong, if, for instance, the person speaks and what we hear is not congruent with what their appearance led us to think. So clothes do convey a message to the world; they reflect the image we wish to project.

Contrary to what you might think, parents do not feel more at ease with teachers in 'casual' clothes; after all they usually dress carefully to come and see you. Children are definitely insulted by 'scruffy' teachers (and on occasion may say so!) They expect you to show that you respect and care for them and the job you are doing.

Dress, then, with common sense and regard for the children and your colleagues. Similarly hair styles should not be too outrageous. The best guidelines are that it should be clean, tidy, not a safety (or health) hazard, and should enable the pupils to see your face clearly when teaching (and also so that you can see them, even peripherally). From my own school days I remember that no-one wanted to sit on the table with the teacher who leaned her head on her hands and scratched over the rice pudding. And, more recently, the student with long hair which, cascading over one eye whenever she bent over a child, meant that she had but one hand with which to help the child, and, just as importantly, she could never see what was going on in the left half of her class. So, save the 'persona' for Saturdays.

Personal study skills

It is probable that you will not need this section if your school or college has already taught you the value of a systematic approach to studying. With time being your most precious commodity on teaching practice, you are well advised to use all possible time saving skills in organising your work. Very briefly, the strategies generally recommended are:

Tackling a text book

A good strategy is SQ3R. This is to *survey* the book quickly; draft some *questions* you expect to be able to answer at the end; *read* for the main ideas, and then re-read; *recall* at the end of each section or chapter; and finally *review* for the accuracy of what you have learned.

The best little book on acquiring study skills in general is *Learn How To Study* by Derek Rowntree. It covers organising your study time: writing essays and note taking and tackling examinations.

A further invaluable habit to acquire now is to keep a record of every book you read. That may sound overwhelming, but it isn't. All you need is a small box of 6×4 inch record cards. Take one for each book you read. Across the top line of the card write, in the following order: author's name and initials; year of publication (note the latest edition, not reprint dates); the title of the book as it appears on the spine, or article; the publisher. If it is an article put the title and editor of the journal in which it appears after the title and before the publisher. This is the agreed academic formula and you will find that this card index system is invaluable when essay or thesis writing and you are required to acknowledge all sources and references. It saves hours of time wondering 'Where did I get that quotation from?' or 'Where did I read that idea on . . .?'. Lists of authorities can quickly be arranged in alphabetical order by shuffling cards. What you put on the rest of the card is up to you. It might be useful to list the chapter headings or contents. Or it may be more useful to note page numbers for references you want to use, or write your own brief comments, even if it's only 'NBG' which at least tells you later that you looked at the book and it's not worth wasting time on again!

This system has served me well for the past fifteen years or so and, once started, it is effortless to maintain.

References

Hargreaves, D. H. (1989). *PGCE Assessment fails the Test*. TES.
HMI (1987). *Quality in Schools*. DES.
ILEA (1986). *Primary School Project*. ILEA.
Rowntree, D. (1988) *Learn How To Study*. McDonald.

'Are you sitting comfortably?'

CHAPTER 2

Are you sitting comfortably?
Then I'll begin

'Homeostasis n. 1. the maintenance of metabolic equilibrium within an animal by a tendency to compensate for disrupting changes. 2. the maintenance of equilibrium within a social group, person, etc.' (Collins English Dictionary)

It is now accepted theory (A. H. Maslow, *Towards a Psychology of Being*) that until the brain's lower order functions such as sleep, thirst, hunger, and warmth, are satisfied, the higher order functions cannot be called into play. This seems fundamental common sense, yet it is not always appreciated by teachers. After all General Booth, founder of the Salvation Army, clearly understood it when he declared 'Feed them first and then talk to their souls. You know for yourself that if you are too cold, or hot, hungry or thirsty, you can't really concentrate on studying or listening.'

'A classroom is an engineered environment'   (Stott)

Physical environment

The first bit of the environment that you can manipulate is the classroom. Check the lighting levels for the lesson. Is it too bright? Are there blinds? Can all the children see what they are meant to be looking at? Do you stand so they can all see you as you address the whole class? Being able to see your face clearly in order to lip read may be critical for a child with even minimal hearing loss. Seeing both you and the board clearly, without either shadow or glare, is critical for a child with poor sight.

Is there enough fresh air to breathe after the last class left? Too low oxygen levels make us sleepy and inattentive, so don't blame the children; open the windows!

Noise is less easily manipulated. You may find yourself in a very noisy classroom; noisy that is, not because of the pupils, but because it is next to the railway, a main arterial road or airport. Or the school kitchen may be next door, in which case you may well have the added sense of smell to contend with. A number of schools have hard thermoplastic floors and chairs with metal legs that are supposed to be cushioned with rubber ferrules. Usually these are nearly all missing, and the din when 30 children stand up, scraping back their chairs is teeth wrenching. Obviously there is little you can do about these situations, except possibly to ask for the chairs to be repaired. The point is for you to be aware of these impediments, then at least you can compensate for them as best you can. Being audible to the class is obviously necessary for all pupils, but it is of especial importance to children with a hearing loss, or a visual impairment as the latter rely heavily on verbal information to compensate for poor sight.

> 'The teacher is the organiser of classroom activity. The teacher sets detailed learning objectives, plans the effective use of time, ensures classroom safety, and arranges the availability of materials.' (DES (1985) *Better Schools*)

The classroom

Before talking about ways in which you can control the physical environment of the classroom, there are one or two observations to be made first.

If you are on teaching practice, then obviously the room is not yours except for short periods. However, many primary teachers with students will encourage you to take part of the room to organise and display work relating to your topic or scheme which may be distinct from general class work.

In secondary schools many rooms are general purpose, others are equipped for specialist subjects such as art, science, cookery, woodwork or drama. The specialist equipment and furniture in these rooms often dictates much of the planning of lessons and activities. This is fine if you are teaching those subjects, but can present great difficulties if you have to teach a subject requiring a fair amount of written work in a room without adequate writing surfaces of the correct height.

As a probationer you may not have a room which is solely yours, in which case it is inconsiderate for your colleagues to set about a radical re-arrangement. Where, however, you do have control then it is up to you to create the sort of working atmosphere you want for your pupils. Stand at the door of the classroom and look in. What first strikes you about it? Does it look inviting, interesting, workmanlike? Is the furniture grouped to allow sensible traffic circulation? Is it clean and tidy, or does it have the appearance of having seen too many battles? It doesn't have to be new, but it should look cared for and well used. Are there interesting and attractive displays of the pupils' work and other features to stimulate interest in what is taught there?

In other words your room should give the immediate impression of a workshop; somewhere where you expect pupils to engage in interesting, purposeful activity. It is up to you to put your personal stamp on it; be it pot plants or pictures, the message should be clear. If your desk and room is a clutter of papers, old or half-finished projects and left-overs, you really are not going to convince your pupils that their work needs to be any different. One of the best art teachers I know has a room that, even when empty, is vibrant with ideas and redolent of the work that goes on there, but there is not a brush or pencil out of place, no left-over bits of paint or clay to be seen. Everything is labelled; all pupils know where things are kept and the procedures for their use. Everyone is expected to clear their own work away at the end of the lesson so that the next class can get straight on with their work. Thus, no time is wasted by anyone on unnecessary hassle, and everyone is creatively employed in the time available. Yet the standard of work produced is outstandingly high, varied and imaginative, and the subject and teacher one of the most popular in the school. What this teacher is also teaching, by example, are good work habits in general, which will certainly be applicable later in the work place.

In considering any re-arrangement of your room several factors must be taken into account. The position of your desk must be where you can see all the class, and it is a base for the children to come for help or monitoring of their work, as well as a collection point for work.

Whether you have single workstations or group them together will depend on the type of activity you plan. You will need to consider the traffic lanes between them and the door, your desk, and any other facilities such as sinks or equipment they may be required to use. Sensible planning removes yet another potential trouble spot for disruptive or dangerous behaviour. Nothing delights the class joker more than the opportunity to make repeated forays to the sink for paint or water, taking the longest route through cramped desks, and wreaking maximum havoc *en route*.

In all kinds of grouping the best teaching is one which takes account of the individual needs within each group and is pitched at the appropriate level in terms of language and materials. Consider your own situation with regard to the age of your pupils and the subject areas you teach. Think about the possible and optimum seating arrangements for them. Do their activities change, making different demands on these arrangements? If so, is it sensible or practical to change the status quo?

The psychological environment and the hidden curriculum

We are all familiar with the phrase 'it's not what you say, it's the way that you say it'. It is well known that you can smile and speak to a dog in honeyed tones, whilst saying something like 'Come here you wretched cur, so's I can cut your head off'. The animal responds to the tone of voice not the content of the message, and approaches fawning and wagging its tail.

The same is true in teaching. I once heard a large teacher fling open his door and bellow at a noisy group of 11 year olds 'Quiet! You sound like a crowd of football hooligans'. The comment more aptly described his outburst than theirs, and certainly did nothing to enhance their respect for him. Indeed it is treatment like this that prompts normally cooperative and courteous youngsters to protest resentfully 'He treats us as though we were idiots'. There should be mutual respect and expectations between teacher and pupils.

It is never more true than in teaching that 'you get what you expect' in terms of both behaviour and standards of attainment — providing, that is, that both are realistic in the first place. If you expect misbehaviour you will get it; if you expect poor work you will get it. A head of art once remarked to a student of the class she was about to teach, 'They're third year remedials. You can't expect much from them, so don't give them the best paper or brushes, they'll only spoil them'. Her expectations were met, of course, for no care had gone into the lesson plan either.

'After all, we are human beans . . .' wrote one child. Yes indeed, and mutual respect, though it may be hard to sustain at times in the face of insolence or abuse, is what you must keep firmly in mind. 'Do as you would be done by', although taught in the scriptures seems to be out of fashion in today's pushy dog-eat-dog society. But even at the lowest level it gets results. Children will always work harder and pay more regard to a teacher who treats them as 'human beans'. That is not to say one who is over friendly or tries to be popular, but someone who is naturally themselves, who shows that they actually *like* children, gets to know them as individuals, and will listen on occasion. Such a teacher also makes it explicitly as well as implicitly clear that they regard what they teach as important and relevant to the child and its world.

How do we make our expectations explicit?

A number of recent reports have expressed concern at what is seen as the low expectations that some schools and teachers have of their pupils. And certainly the sort of view quoted above about lower ability groups is not uncommon if not always expressed so blatantly. Clearly the hidden curriculum – that which is taught, but does not appear on the time table – is of great importance.

Some ways in which we express expectation will be in the first impression we make on our pupils; our own personal appearance (is it clean, tidy and business-like?), the appearance of our classroom (similar criteria); the tone of voice in which we speak to pupils and colleagues. Other clear signals are given by the way we use our eyes in class; when addressing the whole class or a group do you always make sure you are scanning and including everyone in your eye contacts, so that they feel included and involved? When the class is working on its own have you developed the 'eyes in the back of the head' technique which is an essential piece of every teacher's equipment? That is the ability to give attention to one pupil whilst at the same time monitoring the whole class to sense the needs of others or pre-empt any trouble. Is your manner and delivery confident and purposeful, which does not mean bulldozing on regardless, but which does not brook argument or dissent.

Perhaps the most significant way of showing that you respect the work of your pupils is to be meticulous about marking and returning their work on time. Children are very critical of teachers they regard as too 'lazy' or disorganised.

Arrival and dismissal procedures

How many times a day do you receive or dismiss a class? This part of a teacher's life can be one of the most stressful and is often a major worry of students and new teachers. It is certainly one of the keystones of the hidden curriculum in that it sets the tone and makes your expectations clear even before the pupils enter your room. Again, smooth operation is due to good organisation. The first essential is for you to be there, on time, and before the pupils. If this is impossible because you have to come from another class at a distant site, then they must wait quietly outside in the corridor. Make certain that you have all that you and they will need for the lesson ready on your desk before admitting them. Stand in the doorway as they enter. That way you can monitor both the corridor and the room, as well as the speed of flow through the door.

Seating arrangements should have been decided by you (not them) and clearly understood. It is a good idea to have a seating plan of the class with the name of each pupil in your register, especially if you find it hard to learn names. This removes a further potential trouble spot.

In pre-school and year 1 classes it is common practice to have places labelled with the children's names, which serves the additional purpose for them of learning to recognise their names in written form. It is helpful for the teacher because seating plans can be altered to suit different work purposes.

Seating plans themselves are a contentious area. Some would argue for freedom of choice, and friendship groups. For the student and probationer I would strongly advocate that control lies firmly in the hands of the teacher for any one of the six reasons given by Marland against allowing pupils to choose for themselves. Briefly these are, that groups form which may exclude the rest of the class (and you); 'friendship' groups are more likely to be power groups and not in anyone's best interests; 'friends' are not necessarily good for each other in learning situations; individual teaching becomes very difficult for young teachers unable to penetrate closed groups; choice in such matters invariably leads to argument and time is wasted sorting it out and tempers frayed into the bargain. And finally there is your need to know at a glance where everybody is.

Dismissal procedures need to be as carefully planned. Allow ample time for clearing up, collecting work and ending the lesson with a brief summing up of what has been covered, reminders for the next lesson and a courteous dismissal with the room left in good order for the next class. All part of the hidden curriculum of 'how we treat each other'.

The distribution and collection of books and equipment is another area in which you make clear your expectations in the workplace. If every thing is organised and labelled it allows you to give the responsibility to the children for their use, and can be further evidence of your mutual respect in anticipating their sensible behaviour. If this is made quite clear you will not be disappointed. You will also free yourself from many unnecessary clearing up chores, at the same time helping children to realise that someone has to do these things. Less misuse should result. With tighter budgets for books and materials this is a lesson that must be learnt quickly.

Dealing with interruptions

In a busy school there are numerous things to be seen to. Some such as daily registers, dinner money and so on, are administrative and routine. Others such as changes to outings, games fixtures, or lost property are occasional. Nothing disrupts the mood and flow of a lesson more than these important but untimely interruptions. If at all possible do not allow them. I used to have a sign which I hung outside my door 'NO ADMITTANCE. STORY TIME IN PROGRESS'. It worked. If children do come in with messages make them give them to you quietly, and then wait until the end of your lesson to pass them on. Similarly when you plan a lesson that requires a change of activity, and movement round the class, give ample warning and make the procedures that you want followed quite clear.

You will by now have noticed that most of these points are aimed at a smooth uninterrupted flow of work in your classroom, and that is largely dependent on the children being quite clear on the ground rules that pertain in your room. It is basic good classroom management, but it is also one of the most important parts of the hidden curriculum, because you are inculcating good work habits and study skills, regardless of the age or ability of your pupils. With their implementation you should certainly earn a comment on your report similar to: 'The organisation and management of the class were well conceived and were carried out with precision, good humour and common sense.' (*Quality in Schools*)

Engineering the personal requirements of individual children is less easy. You should, of course, establish the ground rules for leaving the class to go to the toilet. With very young children it is wise to make specific times available so that lessons are not interrupted. Very occasionally there are children with specific bladder or bowel conditions which necessitate more frequent trips, but you should be aware of these and agree procedures so that they are not publicly embarrassed, and your lessons are not interrupted.

Some children always appear to be tired, yawning and drooping a lot. Considerable tact is needed here. By careful and gentle questions after a lesson when neither of you is rushed, it might be possible to establish the cause. Most often it is because the child stays up watching late night television, or worse, videos of questionable taste. In such cases a quiet word with a parent, if the child is collected from school, or a courteous note home to the effect that late nights are clearly impairing their child's school work, should be sufficient. Some children from materially disadvantaged homes live in conditions that are far from conducive to a good night's sleep. They may have to share a small bed with younger or older siblings; they may all live in one room, sharing the parents' bed, with no chance of sleep until the parents turn off lights and television for the night.

The personal cleanliness of some of your pupils may be governed by similar circumstances, so be a little circumspect, and make a few discreet enquiries about their backgrounds before you criticise them too harshly. Sexual abuse has received much publicity, and certainly must remain a cause for concern. But if, as a student or probationer, you suspect this in one of your children, *do nothing*. Report your suspicions at once, quietly and confidentially to the teacher who has direct responsibility for the class.

The learning environment

Stott, in his excellent book *Helping Children with Learning Difficulties. A Diagnostic Teaching Approach*, places great emphasis on creating a good learning environment as a prerequisite to meeting the needs of individual children. He takes as his basis what is known about the way children learn, and the optimum conditions under which that learning can take place. From this he proposes ten criteria for assessing the learning environment and suggests they be used in teacher training.

(1) Is the process of learning absorbing and rewarding?
(2) Is there immediate knowledge of success or failure?
(3) Is new learning based on existing capabilities?
(4) Is each pupil able to work at his own level and pace?
(5) Do pupils learn by their own mental activity?
(6) Are there opportunities for peer group learning?
(7) Is time allowed for new knowledge to sink in?
(8) Are the learning situations sufficiently varied?

(9) Is the personal relationship between pupil and teacher conducive to learning?

(10) Are physical conditions conducive to learning?

This chapter has already addressed questions 9 and 10 and elements in some of the others. Chapter 3 deals in more detail with lesson planning, and Chapters 3 and 4 with understanding how children learn and how to meet the needs of the individual.

Raising the standard

In discussing the concerns currently expressed of the need to raise the general standard of education in schools I have suggested that one of the principal ways is by personal good example and high, but realistic, expectations of the children. An integral part of this must surely be in one's own academic standards. How can we expect high standards of work from children if our own command of literacy and numeracy is shaky? If you were unfortunate enough to have gone through primary school with teachers who had the mistaken notion that spelling, grammar, and 'tables' were old fashioned and unnecessary, then you have some repair work to do to prepare yourself to become an effective professional.

There have been too many times when teachers' spelling mistakes on the board and in worksheets have been left for the children to copy. It cannot be too strongly stated that you must not allow this to happen. If spelling is your blackspot, be open, admit it, and *do* something. Note down the words you know you habitually get wrong, and learn them. Do not scorn the use of a dictionary in your preparation of lessons. What you put before children is a model for them by which they set their own standards. It should be factually and grammatically accurate, correctly spelled and legible.

An even more personally sensitive subject is that of accent, dialect, and standard English. It might take some of the emotive heat out of the discussion if some definitions are made.

First, if you are a teacher you are in the communications business. You are required to be able to get over facts, ideas and instructions audibly and clearly. What you say has to be heard and understood. Teaching has a large element of performance in it, so practise is necessary.

Standard English is the accepted language of this country. It is what this book is written in, and what you hear in news broadcasts. It is language that is clear to anyone who understands English. It is not 'posh', 'BBC', or in any way elitist, nor has it much to do with accent. It has accepted grammatical and syntactical structures, although these may be slowly modified with common usage. Therefore as skilled communicators, part of your job is to ensure that your pupils are offered only correct models and helped to acquire a natural and accurate fluency of their own. This does not devalue their own personal accents or dialect, or preclude the use of their own peer and home languages. Indeed in the right place (drama or story telling) these add a valuable richness to their work. In other words, the language of instruction should be in standard English.

Accent is a matter of pronounciation, and matters little, providing you can be easily understood. If you have a regional accent by all means cherish it, but if it is different from the children's, check that it is understood. I recall the distress of a student from Humberside who found she was incomprehensible to her class in Barnsley. With a little modification all was soon well. With another teacher the problem was teaching children to write 'Thursday' and 'Friday' until he realised that his strong south London accent made no differentiation between 'th' and 'f'.

Dialect often differs syntactically and grammatically from standard English, which of course is the root of its charm. 'Where be 'ee to?' is a common phrase heard in Bristol, and 'You can't have it while Tom comes' confuses anyone not from Barnsley where 'while' means 'until'.

Continued and sometimes deliberate misuse of language on radio and television does not help either, as it quickly assumes respectability. One example heard with increasing frequency is 'There are large amounts of people . . .', which conjures up awful images of heaps and piles. 'Amounts' refer to amorphous, inert substances like sand, water, money; whereas 'numbers', to discrete individuals or entities. And 'me and 'im' and 'we was' are also becoming commonplace. To insist on the proper use of language is not being tiresomely pedantic. It is to teach what is correct and accurate. You would not be forgiven (or last long) as a teacher if you were to teach that $3 + 3 = 5$ to a junior class, or that it does not really matter which way round you connect the blue, brown and green wires in an electrical plug. It is interesting to note that it is teachers of science and practical subjects who set store by, and comment on, pupils' literacy skills, for the very reason that their subjects, their 'disciplines', require accuracy of instruction, observation and recording.

A final word on words. We must all have suffered from teachers, lecturers and speakers (even Her Majesty's Inspectors) who may well have had something interesting to say, but we will never know because we could not hear them. This must count as the cardinal sin in teaching. Teaching is performance, and performance needs practice. If you are not sure whether your voice is clear and carries far enough get a friend to listen to you. It is often not just a matter of sufficient volume, but of pitch and projection. Women's voices being, on the whole, higher than men's, tend not to carry so well. A lower pitch properly projected is usually the answer and saves straining the voice, because talking for long periods when you are not accustomed to it is very tiring.

Micro-teaching

Getting a friend to listen to you perform is a non-threatening way of monitoring what you are doing. As you yourself are behind the performance, it is difficult to know how it is coming across, or indeed what else might be going on that you are not aware of.

Another way of monitoring performance in a non-threatening situation is micro-teaching. Many colleges now use this technique, so you may be familiar with it. It consists of a small group of people setting up a short teaching sequence of a few minutes (perhaps to look at different ways of presenting a particular concept). One teaches, others act as students, one observes and records. There is then a short evaluation session where the whole performance is discussed. Then roles are changed and the process repeated. In this way all are in 'the hot seat' in turn and, if done in a constructive atmosphere can be very supportive. If it is possible to obtain the use of a video camera the technique is even more powerful. It is a contrived situation, but it enables students (and tutor) to concentrate on specific aspects of teaching skills, or accomplish certain tasks without the complexities of a whole class, and time taken is reduced. Feedback is immediate, and it also allows for the creation of situations which may occur only infrequently in real life. It should be perfectly possible for students or small groups of probationers in the same school or cluster of schools to arrange a few sessions on their own, and it is one more technique for self-monitoring and appraisal.

32

References

DES (1985). *Better Schools*. HMSO.
HMI (1987). *The New Teacher in School*. DES.
Marland, M. (1976). *The Craft of the Classroom*. Heinemann.
Maslow, A. H. (1968). *Towards a Psychology of Being*. Van Nostrand Reinhold.
Stott, D. H. (1978). *Helping Children with Learning Difficulties*. Ward Lock.

'First catch your pupil.'

CHAPTER 3

First catch your pupil

'An explicit technology of teaching based on our understanding of the conditions for good learning.'
(D. H. Stott, *Helping Children with Learning Difficulties*)

A generation ago Stott identified the biggest advance in education waiting to be made as 'to define those conditions for classroom learning and to build upon them an explicit body of professional practice that can form a major part of teacher training. In short we have to make up our minds what makes for effective teaching.' It would seem that the advance is still incomplete as the HMI second annual report on schools, *Standards in Education*, identified one third of schools as having poor or very poor standards.

Teaching as you were taught?

'Teachers tend to teach as they were taught' is an old truism, reinforced by a pattern of training that attempts to get a gallon into a pint pot. Historically, the one year course was aimed at providing grammar schools with graduates who were presumed to 'know' their subjects, and to teach in the sort of schools they were taught in. What is now needed, of course, are specialist teachers who are also generalists, like primary teachers. At secondary level this is difficult as the level of knowledge over a range of subjects is bound to be fairly superficial. Student teachers, therefore, need to face the fact that they will need to continue to study the content of a range of subjects they are required to teach long after qualifying.

Expanding your repertoire

'Every teacher needs a repertoire of teaching styles . . . Teaching styles have to be varied sensitively to match the nature of the work in hand and the characteristics of the pupils as well as their stage of development'. (*Better Schools*)

As stated earlier we all tend to teach as we were ourselves taught, and for the majority, this was still very much in the 'chalk and talk' tradition. It is, therefore quite difficult to acquire the necessary skills and attitudes to adapt to a whole range of teaching styles.

It's a wise teacher that knows its own child

'Teaching is a complex problem solving activity that never ends' (*Supervision in Teacher Education* by E. Stones). If that doesn't daunt you, read on. Stones also says that 'Psychology is there to be interrogated', which is another way of saying that sound theory should always underpin practice. An important part of this is for all teachers, not only the primary trained, to have a sound knowledge of child development. For it is only when you are aware of the stages of development of children *below* the ages of those you teach, that you will recognise more easily those children who are immature and functioning either emotionally or intellectually below the majority of their peers. This knowledge will then enable you to plan more appropriate strategies and programmes for these pupils, rather than regarding them as 'naughty' or 'stupid'.

Learning versus teaching?

Stott made great advances in identifying a good learning environment, and summarised it in the ten criteria quoted in Chapter 2. There the physical and psychological aspects of the environment were examined. Now, the all important differences between learning and teaching need to be teased out. For what is 'taught', that is, delivered by you, is not necessarily learned by the pupil. An art lesson for remedials will serve to illustrate this.

Imagine a well equipped art room, a 'labelled' class of less able children, and a new teacher who knew her subject thoroughly, but was inexperienced with less able children. Because of their supposed poor ability she had planned a fun lesson where the pupils were to illustrate their favourite television programme in comic strip form. This was reckoned to be of suitable interest to them and not too demanding of their creative skills. They were each given a piece of paper torn from a larger sheet, pencils and crayons which had seen better days and a ruler. Their instructions were to draw ten equal sized boxes with their rulers to represent the comic strip, and then to choose how and what they wanted to illustrate. One boy who she had been told was a trouble-maker was told to sit by himself at the start of the lesson.

Drawing boxes of equal size proved to be the first hurdle, which many never overcame. A suitable choice of 'favourite' required discussion with neighbours, often with dissenting views. Rulers were brought into play to settle some arguments. How to break down a story into ten bite-sized pieces was beyond most of those who got that far.

The 'trouble-maker' did not even attempt the task set, but, in his corner, drew in great detail and with skill his favourite monster without saying a word or leaving his seat all lesson.

At the end of the lesson there was no discussion about the results (some commendable) or the difficulties encountered. Papers were collected. The 'trouble-maker' screwed his forty minutes of concentrated effort into a ball, dropping it, without rancour, in the waste bin on the way out.

It should be possible for you to make some evaluation of this brief account of a lesson using Stott's ten criteria. What, for instance, had the 'trouble-maker' learned in that lesson? What had the teacher actually taught? How much hidden curriculum was there? What skills from other curriculum areas may have been lacking?

What this sad example should point up is the need to examine carefully the theories of *how* children learn and then to consider how to apply them in practice in your lessons with your pupils. What should also be clear is the need to check and double check that:

(1) The children have acquired the necessary basic skills to undertake the task you are setting them.

(2) That what you have taught, or think you have taught, has actually been received, absorbed and understood.

It is useless to go on to something new, or more complex, if they have not. Nor should it be too difficult or time consuming to do this checking if your marking and recording systems are sound. Build into each lesson some time at the beginning to recap on what was done last time and where they had reached, and at the end, recap on the present lesson and give some indication of what to expect in the next. It may sound laborious and time consuming, but it need not be. A few minutes are all that is necessary and the pay-off in terms of steady learning and a good relationship with your class, who see this as proof that you care about their learning, is immense.

Motivation

You can lead a horse to water . . . .

Amongst the many skills required by teachers is the one to recognise and deal with low motivation. They must also foster in pupils the qualities of perseverance and enterprise, together with the abilities to work cooperatively and to accept responsibility.

It is insufficiently recognised that once you have motivated a child to want to know more about something, 'switched her on to something', your task as a teacher is infinitely easier and more rewarding. In turn, the children gain the feeling of being competent and effective, which enhances their self-esteem. Experiences which challenge the intellect, require active participation and use of problem solving skills will most readily promote this learning experience. At the same time class management problems will be minimal, for everyone is too busy to be bothered misbehaving.

Concentration and perseverance

There is currently a dangerous myth put about by television producers of children's programmes that modern children have an attention span of 30 seconds maximum and are incapable of sustaining anything longer. This accounts for the frenetic, fragmented nature of many programmes. That this is pure myth can easily be disproved by anyone watching a very young child absorbed in an activity of their own choosing. It is often the process, not any product, that the child finds rewarding, and this fact is not a bad guide to making our teaching, and their learning, rewarding. Providing the motivation is right, and the task interesting, concentration and perseverance should be no problem.

Lesson planning for key stages 1–4

With the implementation of the National Curriculum, and the recognition that the transition from primary to secondary regime is, at present, too abrupt, methodology for years 6 and 7 needs to be more complementary. Training courses, being specifically primary or secondary, tend to perpetuate the divide of ignorance of the other's best practices. Most attempt to alleviate this in some way by visits to schools in the other phase, but it is consideration of alternative methodologies and strategies that need exploring too in order to ensure the smooth progression of children's learning. The report of the Thames Polytechnic ILEA teachers' course *Fridays Ache My Hands* makes interesting points on this.

Methods are learning experiences placed within a framework of strategies. *Strategies* are the approaches to be used.

This chapter looks at methods suitable for primary and early years' secondary lessons. Strategies, that is what to do for individuals or small groups, is dealt with in more depth in the next chapter.

Aims and objectives

Like 'fish'n chips' and 'bread'n butter', 'aims 'n objectives' are often said as one word, as if there was no difference between them. When it comes to planning lessons the differences should be crystal clear.

Aims are statements of intent. They are philosophical and ethical goals which may be long or short term. They are the *Why* of what you teach.

Objectives are more precisely defined, and observable, goals which, again, may be long or short term for example, by the end of term pupils will have learned that the natural world consists of . . . .

They are psychological and sociological goals. They are the *What* of what you teach.

You are probably familiar with Bloom's hierarchy of learning, which in turn should inform the levels of the objective you set your pupils, and the methods you choose.

$$\left.\begin{array}{ll}\text{knowledge} & \text{level 1} \\ \text{understanding} & \text{level 2} \\ \text{skills} & \text{level 3}\end{array}\right\} \text{the cognitive domain}$$

Higher level objectives fall within the affective domain, and are much more difficult to assess (covering such issues as values and self-expression), although care must be taken not to make the mistake of thinking that because some children are not high achievers in the cognitive domain they are equally poor in the affective areas. The opposite is sometimes true. Stephen Wiltshire's work is an outstanding example.

Objectives should state clearly what the task is, the time in which it should be completed, and the observable outcome in terms of acceptable performance. What is to be done; when; and how well.

A short rule of thumb for assessing objectives you have set might be:

(1) Does it state clearly what is to be done?
(2) Does it describe the conditions under which learning takes place (including time)?
(3) Can we assess progress and performance?
(4) Is it appropriate to the child's levels?

How this all fits into a scheme of work might be summarised as follows:

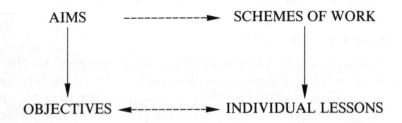

Methods

Whole class

For some reason this seems to have unfashionable connotations, although it is the method still most widely used for older children, and likely to remain so. It has its place in your repertoire of teaching skills; it is the most speedy and efficient way of delivering information to a large group of people, and need not be boring and dull.

Until you are confident about class control and have built up a good relationship with your pupils, it is the best and safest way to learn your craft. All that is necessary for success is good preparation, clearly stated objectives that are known to the children, and a variety of strategies for your presentation. The whole class method operates best for level 1 – cognitive learning – knowledge, although, with practice and skill it can be developed into other areas.

The ILEA *Junior School Project* found that where teachers spend more time in contact with a whole class, higher order communications occur more frequently. These encourage imaginative or problem solving responses.

Groups

In organising the learning environment to accommodate group work the teacher's role changes from central deliverer of information to that of a peripatetic helper and monitor. Remember you are in a more vulnerable position with regard to class control, so the 'eyes in the back of the head', and the ears that can listen to individuals and the general noise level of the class at the same time need to be well developed.

Group work offers opportunities to try out ideas and hypotheses, for cooperative problem solving and discussion, so be sure these are what you have organised to happen. It is often sensible to start with a whole class exposition on the work of the lesson; recapping on previous work covered, and giving new information on which the group work is based.

The groups should be decided by the teacher, not the pupils, and the ground rules for working in them clearly established. Matters such as movement in and between groups, the amount of talking allowed, the use and collection of equipment and so on should all be made plain to the whole class beforehand. Once work has commenced, try to visit each group quickly to encourage and make sure that it is proceeding along proper lines. Note any common problems but do not interrupt the class constantly to draw attention to them. This interrupts their concentration. Save comments to the end, or if there is a gross misunderstanding, stop the whole class, and when you have the attention of everyone, make your point.

The composition of groups needs careful consideration. It is generally best to have a mixture of abilities in each group, so that the less able or slower children can make their contribution to the task at their level. On the other hand it is common practice in primary classes to group children by ability to work at specific aspects of a subject such as maths. Whatever you decide you should be clear about the purpose of the group, and be sure to leave time at the end to bring the whole class together for a follow up session of a few minutes so that they can share experiences, difficulties and triumphs.

It is also common practice in primary class to have groups working on different curriculum areas at the same time in the same class, for instance one table doing maths, another reading, another writing and so on. Research on attainment now shows that the actual performance and attainments of children thus taught are generally lower than those in classes where one curriculum area at a time was being worked on, which surely gives pause for thought in planning activities.

This method affords opportunities for learning at levels 2 and 3 (understanding and skill) to take place, as well as aspects of affective learning. Clearly this method should follow level 1 learning. There has been much criticism that many children observed in group work are not working to capacity either because they do not understand the nature of the task, or do not possess the necessary knowledge to undertake the work.

Mixed ability teaching

One sees a great many mixed ability classes, but not a great deal of mixed ability teaching. However, Reid *et al.* (1982) found that where teachers were involved with it 92% were in favour of it. They saw the perceived advantages to be an avoidance of labelling and a chance to foster personal and social development.

Looking at probationers HMI found that 'In common with many experienced teachers, they found it difficult to cater for the full range of age, ability and experience in the class'. (*Quality in Schools*). HMI go on to point out that although most students were able to discuss individual differences within their class, their actual provision of learning experiences did not reflect those differences. So how is this possible in the limited time available on teaching practice, or in the first year of teaching?

Mini-teaching

There may be opportunities during serial practice to work with small groups of children with a specific objective such as studying individual differences and how to cater for them in specific curriculum areas. In this way it is possible to focus on such issues as rates of progress and levels of work, and then to reflect and plan appropriate strategies or programmes of work for a range of abilities to be tried out in subsequent sessions. In many ways this is better than the usual practice of having lectures and discussions on mixed ability teaching and no opportunity to get to grips with any solutions practically when faced with teaching a whole class.

A further way to develop your teaching skills quickly on teaching practice is to work with another student and a group of children to teach a specific practical skill. One student teaches; the other observes. Then positions are reversed, and at the end of the lesson both can comment on their observations, analyses and evaluations. This works well for physical education and other practical activities like drama, music, dance, art, craft, science and homecrafts.

Presentation skills

Explanations

Clarity and fluency are essential to effective teaching. Verbally this means the apt use of words, and grammatically correct sentences without hesitations or redundancies – 'erm', 'y'know', and 'I mean' – the crutches with which many people stumble through their thoughts.

Visual clarity can often be more easily achieved through diagrammatic representation than by the use of words. The following flow diagram attempts to explain the whole process of planning explanations by just such means.

EXPOSITIONS

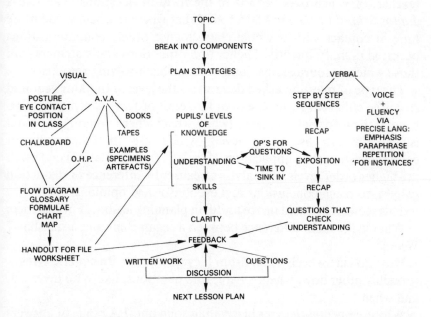

Check your schemes and lesson plans against the diagram above. It may look onerous; it is not. Not all points need to be used equally. Some need only a few seconds to check. Follow the preacher's edict.

Tell 'em what you're going to tell 'em.

Tell 'em.

Tell 'em what you've told 'em.

Questioning

> Questioning demands a range of techniques ranging from the closed question that calls for a single precise answer to the open ended question which encourages different avenues of thought and speculation... Cultivating communication and independent learning means that pupils must be put into situations where they can explore lines of thought, set up hypotheses, and develop reasoning powers... Pupils should be encouraged to form opinions supported by evidence, to defend those opinions by logical argument and careful expression, and to recognise that in many situations more than one opinion can reasonably be held. (*Better Schools*)

An important part of the teacher's repertoire is the ability to establish and nurture good classroom relationships which permit and encourage these developments.

What is this range of questioning skills? In general questions should enable and teach rather than test.

Studies have shown that a startling 72% of classroom talk is by the teacher, of which over 90% is in the form of questions! The ILEA *Junior School Project* has also found that where teachers spend more time in contact with a whole class 'higher order' communications occurred more frequently. Higher order questions and statements are those which encourage imaginative or problem-solving responses.

The type of question asked determines the level of thinking required from the children. From lower order recall of facts which do not go beyond the information given, (who? what? when? where?) the pupil is led through ascending levels which use thinking skills of comprehension, then application of 'rules', (how? what if?) and on to the higher order levels of analysis of causes by inference or deduction (why?), to reach conclusions and even informed opinions.

This sequence should prove useful in planning lessons. For instance:

What is the main difference between a sedan chair and a rickshaw? Wheels.

How do cart wheels differ from bicycle wheels? Pneumatic tyres. (Possibly other how, when, where, who questions, like Who invented, and when.)

Why are pneumatic tyres better than solid ones? A range of answers possible.

This ability to make connections between previous disparate 'bits' of knowledge, until what Koestler called the Eureka! response is evoked – the 'Ah ha, *now* I get it!' – is at the core of the joy of learning. Questions should not be guessing games of 'what is teacher thinking?'.

If incorrect answers are given do not say 'No, that's wrong'. This is a put down, and can be quite damaging to the self-esteem of a timid child. Ask a further enabling question which gives a little more information or approaches the subject from a different angle, and provokes thought and problem solving. This is possible even with closed questions. For instance, if a wrong answer is given to the question 'What is two and two?' you can still reply 'Just a minute. A dog has two legs at the front and two at the back. How many legs has he?'

Do not repeat a question (unless it has not been heard properly). Re-phrase it so that its meaning is clearer.

A final thought on questions. If *you* are at the receiving end of a question you can't answer, be honest and admit you do not know – but you do know where *we* can find out and learn together.

Language across the curriculum

> The complex rules governing the combination of elements when we speak or write impose order upon the experiences we succeed in putting into words.
>
> (Bullock, *A Language for Life*)

Those of you trained for early years will be familiar with the stages of language development. The new born's random sounds have by six months become babble which is recognisably that of the parent's language. Phonemes of that language soon appear, followed by words, and portmanteau phrases such as 'Dinner allgone'; 'daddy allgone'. Then come simple sentences and finally discourse.

It is clear from listening to young children that language acquisition is not haphazard, but governed by grammatical rules. Children display an innate awareness of these, as illustrated by the three-year-old's 'I've tooken a apple'. The exceptions to these rules are acquired from adults teaching them. Thus standard English or a variety of dialect is learnt. Although the latter may have particular words and syntax peculiar to itself – 'Shall we put us coats on?' and 'The shop is open while six' – it is still governed by rules of grammar.

Jargon is words and phrases which are exclusive to a subject or group. It is important for specialist teachers to recognise this and positively teach these words and phrases *before* expecting children to understand and use them. It is all too easy to assume that children understand the exact meanings of words such as 'file' in all their different contexts. Do you mean storing papers, smoothing nails, metalwork, standing in line, a computer term – all are possible in different curriculum areas. In the main jargon is best avoided, for when used to excess it becomes meaningless gobbledegook.

Register your personal language map; the way you speak differs according to your audience, and it is something of which a teacher should be conscious. For instance, think of the last three occasions you spoke to different people; a friend or family member; a phone call to order something; a busy shop assistant; your class; a group in the playground, and so on. A moment's reflection will show that you used very different styles of speech to suit the different occasions and audiences. So for different teaching methods and subjects you will need to be conscious of the need for clarity and precision.

The diagram (on p. 47) illustrates the components of language and *the order in which they are acquired by the child*. This aspect of teaching is frequently overlooked, but it is important for it should dictate your levels of teaching and the demands and expectations you have of each child. It is obvious from the diagram that it is unreasonable to expect a child who has not yet learned to speak with any coherence, and lacks listening skills, to start to learn to read, especially if he has little or no experience of books and their function. The idea that squiggles on paper may actually convey a message (and even be exciting) and relate to sounds made in talking, that words are discrete entities and so on, is for many children light years away from the everyday experiences they bring to school.

This does not mean, however, that because a child is not verbally fluent he cannot begin to learn to write, and similarly he cannot begin to learn to read until he can write fluently. As the diagram shows, all must run along in parallel, but with the earliest skill leading. This continues to hold true for many older children with learning delays, and should be recognised in planning their work.

Language and learning in the secondary school

This principle is frequently overlooked by secondary teachers of specialist subjects who sometimes attempt to introduce concepts in advance of the language abilities of their pupils.

Scientific, mathematical and other specialist languages must be consciously taught, as common words may have totally different and specific meanings in their separate discipline contexts. For instance, tree, root, branch and file in computing, seed, cell and solution in chemistry, biology and mathematics.

THE ACQUISITION OF LANGUAGE SKILLS

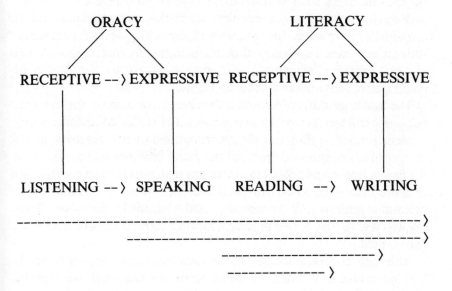

Equal opportunities education

The Government White Paper *Better Schools* expresses concern at the under-achievement of many pupils from ethnic minorities, but points out that such groups are relatively more affected by social and economic disadvantage which is likely to account for much of their under-achievement. It also notes, and deplores, the racial harassment that many are subjected to. It highlights the responsibility of teachers and schools to give priority to the teaching of English to these pupils, and to address, through the curriculum and attitudes in the school, the promotion of racial tolerance and harmony.

There is a subtle, but real, difference between multi-ethnic and multi-cultural which should be clearly understood. People from the same country or subcontinent may share ethnic origins, but have quite diverse cultures. Sikh, Muslim, Hindu and Christian cultures, for instance, are a case in point.

The equal opportunities issues of race, sex and disability are now enshrined in law, and schools must be seen to carry a heavy responsibility in instilling the tolerant acceptance of the rich diversity of peoples in our society.

There are numerous and exciting ways of working on this; children's literature is a treasure chest of opportunities; schools which are fortunate in having a cultural mix provide opportunities to involve families in topics such as festivals of light, food, dress and customs. The obvious curriculum areas here are dance, drama, music, home economics, as well as history, geography and religious education. Indeed, the new regulation that all primary teacher courses must include religious education will give a boost to the study of comparative religions and broaden horizons.

The language differences and difficulties must also be appreciated, for many children arrive in our schools with little or no understanding of basic English. This is not always recognised by new teachers, nor is the cultural background from which many children come, widening the gap in home and school expectations which so frequently give rise to unnecessary problems for the child. For instance in some male-orientated cultures, it is not expected that little boys will dress themselves, so they arrive at school lacking those skills which we take for granted.

Although the race section of the law on equal opportunities is highlighted here, it should be remembered that the other two aspects, gender and disability, are equally important in balancing your teaching.

Summary

The chapter analyses the elements of effective teaching; the differences between learning and teaching and the importance of applying learning, motivational and child development theories to practice. In lesson planning the importance of distinguishing between methods and strategies, and aims and objectives is stressed. Methods for whole class, group, mixed ability, practical team teaching and transitions are covered. Presentation skills include explanations, questioning, the use of equipment and the pacing of lessons, the importance of language in teaching and learning, as well as its impact on various aspects of the curriculum, are dealt with.

References

Bloom, B. S. (1956). *Taxonomy of Educational Objectives*. Longman.
Bullock, A. (1975). *A Language for Life*. HMSO.
DES (1985). *Better Schools*. HMSO.
HMI (1987). *Quality in Schools*. DES.

HMI (1990). *Standards in Education*. DES.
ILEA (1987). *Fridays Ache My Hands*. ILEA/Thames Polytechnic.
ILEA (1986). *The Junior School Project*. ILEA.
Kerry, T. (1982). *Effective Questioning*. Macmillan.
Koestler, Arthur (1978). *Janus*. Hutchinson.
Reid, M. *et al.* (1982). *Mixed Ability Teaching*. NFER/Nelson.
Stones, E. (1984). *Supervision in Teacher Education*. Methuen.
Stott, D. H. (1978). *Helping Children with Learning Difficulties*. Ward Lock.
Wiltshire, S. (1988). *Drawings*. Dent.

'*We're all human beans.*'

CHAPTER 4

Exploding the myth of the normal child

'The mind becomes what it does' *Overstreet.*

What do we mean by 'normal'? The dictionary defines it as 'usual, regular, common, typical'; that is, without defined limits. Or, 'as being within certain limits of intelligence, educational success or ability'. A normal curve of distribution is a symmetrical bell shaped curve with equal tails. It can be used to show the theoretical distribution of intelligence in a population. The point around which the largest number of people are to be found is deemed the 'norm' and given the figure of 100. This is calculated from the formula *Mental Age* divided by *Chronological Age* × 100 = Intelligence Quotient.

$$\frac{MA}{CA} \times 100 = I.Q.$$

The majority of children fall between 85 and 115.

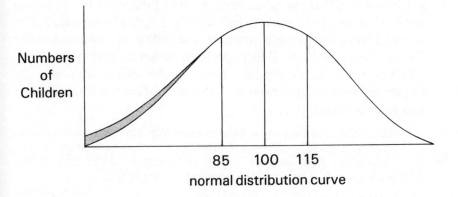

normal distribution curve

However, three important points should be borne in mind.

(1) These figures are derived from one set of measures; standardised tests, which are now acknowledged to be impossible to make culture-free. Other factors are personality and health. These can affect performance and attainment far more significantly than general intelligence.

(2) It should be noted that the curve does not adhere to the theoretical model, but is skewed to the lower tail. 'Intelligence' is largely determined in embryo and cannot subsequently be raised by more than a few points. However, a number of subsequent events can lower it. Injury before, during, and after birth can result in brain damage, as can disease and the effects of drugs, all of which impair the functioning of the brain.

(3) Intelligence tests are a dipstick in time. They measure, by their own criteria, the *present* level of functioning at a particular moment. It is important, therefore, to know the date a test was administered, and the *age of the pupil* at that time. Any use or evaluation of these results must be made in the light of these circumstances. Given a good educational environment at home or school intelligence can improve in children. It is not immutable.

For example, it is quite likely that you will encounter in your classes a child of 10 with a mental age (as calculated from the results of standardised tests) of 13, and another of the same age with an MA of 7, giving IQs of 130 and 70; both outside the 'norm'.

Given this far from black and white picture, at what point do you decree the end of 'normality' and set a limit, below which children are labelled 'sub-normal', or above which they are considered 'super-normal'? Do we need limits? In the lives of real children is it helpful to be labelled at all? It has taken until the 1981 Education Act to decree that it is not, and to re-assert in legislation the right of *every* child to be educated 'according to age, aptitude and ability' as enshrined in the 1944 Act and now in the Education Reform Act of 1988 (ERA).

This is not to ignore the fact that a number of children have, by accident of birth or circumstance, a range of difficulties which impede their rates of learning.

> All teachers . . . need to be able to recognise when the reason for an individual pupil's poor performance lies elsewhere than in low motivation, poor preparation or presentation of lessons, or the teacher's failure to adapt to the mood of the class.
>
> *Better Schools*

There is a whole range of reasons why a child may not be able to perform as well as his or her peers. They may have poor hearing or eyesight, asthma, heart or other medical condition which may be intermittent, temporary or permanent. Or they may have genuine learning or emotional problems which interfere with normal learning.

These reasons are not always known to the school or teacher, let alone recognised. Whilst not every teacher is an expert on special educational needs, every teacher ought to have enough ability to recognise the symptoms of difficulty, and to know where to get further specialist help. As it is fairly certain that most teachers will have pupils with special needs in their class, it is strongly recommended that every school has a designated teacher with responsibility for coordinating the assessment, recording and provision for special needs within the school. This should be a head of department or unit in a secondary school, or a senior teacher in a primary school. Make sure you know who it is.

Special educational needs and initial training courses

The 1987 HMI survey of teacher training is extremely critical of the variety and levels of courses offered to students, despite the requirement since 1984 for *all* initial training courses to contain an 'element' of awareness on Special Educational Needs (SEN). Some are reasonable in length and breadth, others merely token. Where SEN is offered as an option (albeit often well constructed and taught), 'it is possible for many students to devote little or no time to this essential aspect of training'. They call for much more substantial courses occupying a larger part of professional studies, on the easily justified grounds that 'good teaching for SEN means good teaching for *all* children'.

My own experience with probationary teachers from all over the country bears this out. Some were well grounded and reasonably confident, others theoretically aware but had not been taught *what* to do in the classroom, whilst others were very conscious that they lacked even a basic awareness of the area.

The range of special educational needs

The Warnock Report *'Special Educational Needs'* was the first complete survey of provision for children with handicaps. Its main proposals (now enshrined in the 1981 Education Act) were to abolish the categories of handicap, based as they were on medical and psychological models that did not define an educational need. It clearly and boldly stated that the aims of education were to be the same for all children:

> The goals are two-fold ... to enlarge a child's knowledge, experience and imaginative understanding, and thus his awareness of moral value and capacity for enjoyment; and secondly, to enable him to enter the world when formal education is over as an active participant in society and a responsible contributor to it, capable of achieving as much independence as possible. The educational needs of every child are determined in relation to these goals.

Given that strong statement it followed logically that cut off points for 'normal' and 'subnormal' were redundant. Once the notion of a continuum of ability–disability was accepted it was no longer important to pursue the will o' the wisp of measuring intelligence *per se*. The needs of the individual were to be paramount. The inevitable corollary is an acceptance of a continuum of provision to accommodate the variety of individual needs. The wherewithal to implement this counsel of perfection is still the subject of much debate and contention, especially as other priorities are declared which compete for scarce funds.

How do we identify those with special educational needs? And, having identified them, how and what do we teach in order to minimise or remove those difficulties?

The Warnock Report stated that besides the identified 2% of children then in special schools catering for categories of handicap, there were around 20% of the mainstream school population that had varying degrees of special need, ranging from mild, short term and transitory, to long term, often chronic and undiagnosed difficulties that the school system were failing to meet. It has since been agreed that in a few deprived inner city schools the proportion of needy children can be as high as 40%, even by the strictest criteria.

What causes special educational needs?

It is probably easiest to define difficulties in terms of either physical, learning, or behavioural. Of course it should always be remembered that children are complex creatures and may well have a mixture of one, two or all of these groups! These inter-relationships of cause and effect are represented by dotted lines in the diagram opposite.

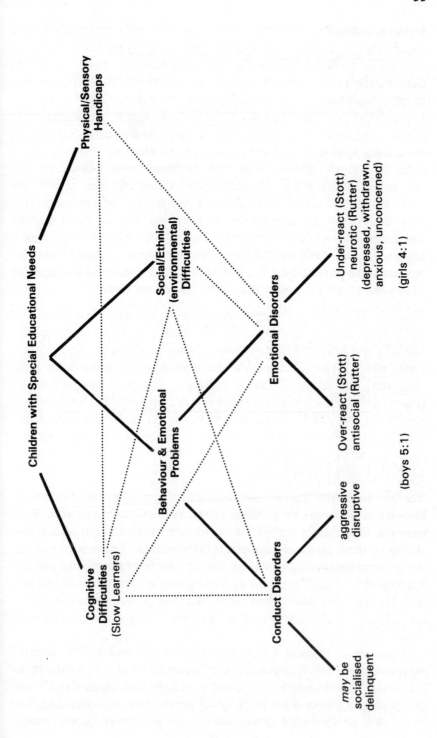

Children with Special Educational Needs

Cognitive Difficulties (Slow Learners)

Physical/Sensory Handicaps

Social/Ethnic (environmental) Difficulties

Behaviour & Emotional Problems

Emotional Disorders

Conduct Disorders

Over-react (Stott) antisocial (Rutter)

Under-react (Stott) neurotic (Rutter) (depressed, withdrawn, anxious, unconcerned)

aggressive disruptive

may be socialised delinquent

(boys 5:1)

(girls 4:1)

Physical difficulties

1 Conditions affecting the central nervous system

Cerebral Palsy It is important to remember that this birth condition spans a similar continuum to SEN, from very mild to totally disabling. It may be slight, affecting only a limb and producing mild spasticity, tremors, unsteady gait or a speech defect. At the other extreme is quadriplegia, where both arms and legs are affected, speech may be unintelligible or absent, and the paralysis may extend to the intellectual functioning of the brain. Obviously the effects on classroom performance will vary with the severity of the condition. Help may only be needed in handwriting, or in PE exercises encouraging the child to use the weaker side, or with practical skills. More severe cases will need more physical help in consultation with the parents and a physiotherapist. Basically, CP affects mobility, balance, handwriting, spatial awareness, orientation, and speech.

Epilepsy The British Epilepsy Association estimate that 1 in 200 children in England and Wales have a form of epilepsy and the vast majority are educated in mainstream schools. There are four forms, one of which is rare. Teachers should be aware of the other three, their symptoms and likely effects on children. The most severe form is Grand Mal (tonic–clonic); the other two are Petit-Mal (absences which are fleeting but maybe frequent, and result in the child missing a few seconds of a lesson), and psychomotor or temporal lobe (complex partial). The BEA have produced an excellent teachers' pack including a poster showing what to do if someone has a fit.

The 'clumsy child' This is now a recognised syndrome, though little is known about its cause; it is thought to be a mild form of brain damage, resulting in a child's inability to orientate which in turn affects the ability to read, write or coordinate movements. There may well be connections here with dyslexia (in the strictest sense), and with specific learning difficulties. This is the child who always seems to have two left feet, always confuses left and right, and who genuinely cannot make his body obey verbal commands or copy visual directions in an activity lesson.

There are a number of *degenerative conditions of the central nervous system* which can occur in children. Most are mercifully rare, but their effects *lessen* the child's ability and potential. Their psychological effects must be fully appreciated by all concerned, for such a child needs skilled counselling to cope with the tragic realisation that as his friends grow and gain skills in leaps and bounds, his own are diminishing.

Genetic abnormalities The best known of these abnormalities is *Downs Syndrome*. This too ranges from near normal appearance and ability to the most profound mental handicap.

2 Muscular and skeletal abnormalities

These include such conditions as *spina bifida*, *muscular dystrophy* (which mainly affects boys), and *cystic fibrosis* (which has related respiratory problems requiring regular physiotherapy), and a number of childhood heart and lung conditions. Teachers should be told if they exist in children in their care, so that they may take sensible precautions to see that those children do not overtire or strain themselves unduly, whilst at the time continuing to treat them in the same way as their peers.

3 Other medical conditions

Diabetes There has recently been an unexplained increase in the number of children with *diabetes mellitus*, the childhood form of the disease which can require life-long insulin injections. The increase is reported to be from 8 per 100,000 in 1973 to 13 per 100,000 in 1988. From the teacher's point of view the main thing to watch for is that the child has taken the prescribed medication. Without it sudden diabetic coma can result, or if the child needs food, his behaviour can become characteristically hyperactive and aggressive. Such children need regular snacks to maintain a steady balance in blood sugar levels. Teachers should know of these requirements, and ensure they are met.

Asthma and associated allergies These conditions are often inherited, and, except in the severest cases, are unlikely to pose problems for the teacher. In most cases the condition is well controlled by drugs which the child is taught to self administer with an inhaler. However, exposure to grass, pollens, and other irritants can severely limit a child's outdoor activities. Good posture and correct breathing can help to maximise lung capacity and is of long term benefit.

All chronic medical conditions in children can result in absences from school. These may be short but frequent or prolonged and involve hospital stays. It is often the former, which tend to go unremarked, that can have the most deleterious effects on performance in class and general attainment levels. Intermittent absence is *the* most disruptive factor in a child's learning process, prejudicing continuity and progress. constant illness or feeling under par is ver debilitating. Unless the child is well-motivated, this can quickly result in such a gap from his peers that he becomes alientated from the whole educational process. A sensitive teacher can do much to prevent this happening.

Language impairment

The main channel of communication between people is by the spoken word. A child who cannot understand the spoken word (receptive language), or cannot make himself understood through speech (expressive language), will have enormous problems of communication and learning. Additionally, language impairment may also affect emotional and social growth unless specific help is given by specialist teachers and speech therapists. A small number of such children have additional severe behavioural problems, and may be termed 'autistic'. They require very specialised teaching.

Sensory impairments

Hearing

This is well named 'the invisible handicap'. Again these conditions run the whole range from a mild hearing loss to total and profound deafness. Children with profound hearing loss need special systems of teaching and are usually taught in special units with as much integration with their peers as possible. But in every school there are large numbers of children, many of them undiagnosed, with varying degrees of hearing loss.

All teachers, therefore, should appreciate the difficulties of these children, for it cannot be too strongly stated that minimal intermittent hearing loss will cause learning delays. If you suspect a child of having this difficulty a crude test is to call their name when they are not facing you. The commonest cause of this kind of hearing loss is 'glue ear' (*otitis media*), an infection of the middle ear which is exacerbated in the winter when colds and 'flu are prevalent. The degree of loss varies with the state of the infection, so it is often difficult to pin point, especially as many children go to great lengths to conceal these difficulties. Obviously if a young child is not hearing clearly they are not easily going to make the vital distinctions between speech and letter sounds which are necessary to acquire speech and reading.

Typical errors are omissions of word endings and the plural 's'. Also, as you will have experienced yourself, if listening is a strain, then you tire quickly and tend to 'switch off'. Intermittent hearing equals intermittent learning.

Some compensation for this can be made by reinforcing learning through the stronger communication channel of sight. Clear visual presentation of material will greatly help to correct faulty information gained aurally.

Visual impairment

Children without any usable sight are taught by non-visual means, including braille, but there are many children with a range of visual problems in the ordinary school. Providing they wear their spectacles, (and many are reluctant to do so) there should be few difficulties for them. The teacher should take care to be audible, and to position himself where his face and chalkboard are clearly visible. If possible, changing the pupil's place in class to avoid shadow or glare from a window will help. Children with more severe visual impairment need printed materials that are clear, in heavy type and with unambiguous illustrations. Worksheets should be particularly well prepared and presented. A pale, smudged sheet will not do.

HIV positive children. *Aids and drug-related conditions* are, sadly, new categories of illness. In 1989 there were already 70 children with the Aids virus in schools in Scotland, but no figures are available as yet for England and Wales. It is an inescapable fact, however, that there are numbers of children now being born with such infections passed on in the womb, or with brain damage resulting from drug abuse. These children have the same rights of access to education as everyone else.

There may be other conditions you encounter during your teaching career, but the basic rules are the same. Commonsense and sensitivity to a child's changing needs and physical condition (tiredness, irritability), plus *essential* information from home and the doctor, must govern your teaching approach. There is no justification for withholding such essential information which affects classroom performance from the teacher(s) most directly concerned with the child's education, for childhood occurs but once and is brief.

School-created and school-related causes

It is increasingly being recognised that the 'problems' related to special educational needs often lie not within the child, but the school, and it is for schools to solve these problems by changing their attitudes and practices, not the children who must change. The children just *are*: they come to school by law and arrive with all the miscellaneous personal baggage that everyone carries with them, and that is how we must accept them. Children have always needed, and will continue to need, all the help they can get from committed teachers with compassion and vision.

As *'A Curriculum For All'* states, it has taken years for the principle of 'entitlement' to gain acceptance and become statute, but ensuring 'access to the curriculum' is another matter. It will depend on a change of attitude and practice in schools which can be hastened by new teachers bringing those attitudes and skills with them.

There are still schools who deny the existence of children whom they regard as less than wholesome, as though to do so was some reflection on their teaching ability! This is not such an uncommon attitude as you might suppose. Others, usually secondary schools, sigh for the 'good old days' (whatever they were), and continue to offer indigestible and outmoded menus that are swallowed with difficulty by the majority, let alone pupils with learning or behavioural difficulties. These latter children are offered a thin gruel, an unappetising, watered down curriculum that fails to nourish, and sometimes it is totally rejected, accounting for the high drop out rate above year 10.

How do I identify a child with learning difficulties?

In general the characteristics of such a child are:

- poor motivation
- a short attention span
- a poor memory
- possibly below average physique
- delay in reading and possibly in spoken language and maths
- often has minor physical or sensory impairments
- *low self-esteem*

Do not blame them for these deficits. Your teaching must be aimed at overcoming them as far as possible.

Let us examine more closely some of these points.

If their learning difficulties are truly due to low intelligence, then some of the following points *may* apply, but take care not to make assumptions too readily.

These children do badly in academic tasks, seeking out routine jobs and preferring practical work. Their records show that they are often clumsy in PE and craft work. They are poor attenders, often late and with poor attitudes to school. They may have had several changes of school, and possibly be known to the schools' psychological service.

Intellectually they are very limited with little curiosity, and general knowledge, few interests, have difficulty in following instructions, and contribute little in discussion. They are equally limited verbally, with a poor vocabulary, speaking only in short responses, often only single words, although paradoxically they are sometimes inconsequential chatterboxes. They are often the maddening child who will attend to everything except the job in hand!

Physically they may seem small for their age, have a speech impediment or defective vision or hearing; lack coordination and be messy, disorganised and clumsy.

Socially they are frequently outcasts or loners, and, being on the fringe, may be aggressive or disruptive.

Emotionally immature they often have a poor self-image, be anxious, restless, have tantrums and be moody and withdrawn.

Their family backgrounds may include disadvantages such as unemployment.

This may seem a dismal litany of negative features, but it is to be hoped that no single child will present more than a few of them. Its purpose is to give you some sort of a brief checklist when looking at the ability range in your class. It should by now be clear that there are many characteristics listed that have already been mentioned in connection with hereditary and physical *causes*. It should also give you pointers to the possible origins of some behavioural disorders.

What next?

Your next step is a happier one. It is to list against the downside, all the positive attributes of the child; his strengths, talents, interests, personality traits and so on, for it is on these that you must build. Just as it is cheering to remember that no class is wholly bad all the time, so with each child.

A further useful diagnostic tool is one devised by Stott to be used as a preliminary screening of the class to discover children's learning styles. It uses a three point scale of 'definitely', 'sometimes' and 'never' against statements as applied to each child. These are:

● Shows by his answers that he is giving attention
● Copes with new tasks without getting anxious or upset

- Settles to an activity and concentrates
- Is willing to join the activities of the group
- Will 'have a go' on his own
- Will accept help when necessary
- Is an alert child who shows interest in activities

There are no formal scores; the cut off point for concern should be decided in the light of your knowledge of the cultural and social background of the school as a whole. It is claimed that a survey of a class of thirty can be done in under an hour – a consideration when time is one's most precious commodity. The underlying principle of this diagnostic teaching approach is that a child does not have an 'intellectual deficit' but employs faulty strategies to his learning; a much healthier and more constructive attitude to teaching.

How do I accommodate my teaching to these needs?

Just as students must acquire study skills, so children must acquire learning skills. The majority of children come to school ready to learn. Some, however, do not, and if they do not 'learn how to learn' early in life the problem is quickly compounded.

These are aspects of teaching that HMI, and all teachers, acknowledge as being the most complex, hence the claim in the NCC document '*A Curriculum For All*' that what is good practice for SEN is good practice for all.

Young teachers who start with the best intentions are often overwhelmed by these complexities. In order to simplify the process let us re-examine the learning model discussed in Chapter 3, for that can give a framework for strategic planning.

The sequence of the learning process runs:

AROUSAL→ATTENTION→MOTIVATION→LEARNING
PHASE→INTEGRATION (VIA REHEARSAL)→MEANING AND
INTENTION→MEMORY.

As this shows the learning process starts well before the learning phase, which is where most programmes start. But if these earlier steps have not been taken, then the rest does not follow effectively.

To return to the key question 'But what do I do?' try the following:

(1) Using the information from these indicators, your knowledge of the child and the possible causes of difficulty, *identify* the main faulty learning style the child has, and tackle that. *Don't* try to solve them all at once!

(2)   Use the sequence of learning model to see where this fault occurs, as it is simpler to devise a remedial strategy.

Arousal First check homeostasis (Chapter 2) for physical aspects. Is the child on medication that may cause drowsiness? Is the task boring – from the child's point of view? (How many times have you nodded off in lectures?) The 'surprise packet' often works wonders. The use of provocative pictures and material is a marvellous stimulus. (And by provocative I don't mean pornographic or page 3!) Pictures or objects, Russian nesting dolls, for instance, that are not what they seem provoke curiosity and comment. News magazines are a good source. I kept a collection which included a lady painted to look like part of the tree she was in; a back view of a fat man on a park bench between two baby elephants; a steeple jack, and so on. Funny and provocative, they provided the starting point for a number of lines of teaching.

Attention and motivation Without doubt these are the key to successful learning; the 'wanting to learn' element. A child may be sluggish and difficult to arouse, or distractible and impossible to keep on-task. Short tasks with built in instant success are needed initially. With all children the value of play activities are the most effective. Other advantages of a 'play' situation is freedom from anxiety over consequences. It doesn't matter if you don't win; there is always another opportunity. Utilise these features of play in constructing activities that are self rewarding, and of interest to the child. The underlying principles of play are applicable to any age, and should not be ignored just because the pupil is of secondary age. The power of intermittent reinforcement should also be harnessed (as any gambler will testify, it is the chance of the odd win which keeps them at it).

Gamesmanship

Small group games provide excellent contexts for increasing the attention span of hyperactive chidren. They also allow them to learn by observation of other's attempts; to have time between turns to rehearse answers; and to explore a problem without committing themselves until they feel safe to do so. A further advantage of games is that any amount of repetition can take place without it becoming boring. This incidentally takes in a further stage in learning – the need to rehearse and repeat a skill before it becomes understood and internalised.

Of course the selection and construction of such games needs to be considered very carefully. Most commercial board games reinforce the wrong things. The rules are complicated; there are winners and losers, and so on. Stott's *Flying Start* materials may now be considered old-fashioned, but if available are worth looking at for the sound principles they incorporate. There are now numerous educational games on the market, but scrutinise them carefully, making sure they meet the learning criteria outlined. Choose ones for a specific learning point; do not fall into the trap of using them as time fillers or educational dummies, to keep the children quiet. It is not difficult, once those principles are grasped, to construct games which are appropriate for your own children. (Drake Educational specialise in educational materials for children with SEN.) The time thus spent will save you many hours of frustration in the future, as well as freeing you to give attention to others knowing that your slow learners are actively learning without your immediate attention.

For example, to teach the recognition and naming of colours make a die with each face a different colour. On a board draw a curving track of differently coloured boxes or cells. Teacher and child take turns to throw the die and move it to the matching box, naming the colour. As soon as the game is understood another child takes the teacher's place. Later the colour word can be added on the boxes and so on.

Similar simple counting games can be made. The nursery rhyme 'Incy wincy spider' can be used to teach taking turns, the concepts of 'up' and 'down', as well as simple counting. You will need a die and a board with the spider at one end and the rain at the other, and a line across the middle of a vertical ladder. Starting with one counter on the centre line, two players take turns to throw the die and move the counter towards their goal (the rain washing the spider down; the spider climbing up). 'Plus', 'minus', and negative numbers can also be taught by the same game used horizontally as the rope in a tug o' war.

Once the concepts are grasped it is not difficult to make or choose material suitable for any age or ability.

Songs and nursery rhymes are rich teaching sources as well as being a part of our cultural heritage. The reason so many old rhymes have survived is precisely because of this value. Children enjoy anticipating the line endings of well known rhymes such as 'There was an old woman who lived in a...' which, besides training anticipation, prediction, and focusing attention, also develops listening and language skills. Older children enjoy more sophisticated versions, composing their own nonsense verse and the ultimate in limericks

There was a young man of St Bees
Who was stung on the leg by a wasp.
When asked 'Does it hurt?'
He replied 'No, not much'
'But I'm glad it wasn't a hornet.'

If low self-esteem is a problem for a child, it is possible to devise activities that give instant success, but this largely depends on the steps and levels being balanced between not too hard and yet sufficiently challenging. They should also be self-correcting for two reasons. The child does not have to wait for you to tell him if it is right or not, and so face is saved and confidence built up. For instance, cards which have to be paired (say simple arithmetical equations) can be colour coded on the backs. The child soon realises that there is no point in 'cheating' for he is not competing with anyone but himself.

Task analysis of the learning process

This simply means breaking your teaching down into steps that children can easily manage. Contrary to what you might think, this does not slow down either your coverage of the syllabus, or the children's learning. Indeed it has the opposite effect, by providing constant successful experiences, which in turn generate an eagerness for more. Remember, *nothing succeeds like success*!

Rehearsal

Opportunities for this have already been mentioned in game playing. They can also be given through short sessions of mental arithmetic, spelling and table bees and in the group and class discussion. Whatever is chosen, there needs, somewhere in the day, to be time for reflection by the children, as well, of course, as your recapping of the ground recently covered in a topic or lesson.

Meaning and intention

These will have been attained through the above strategies if they were designed to match the pupils' 'real world' knowledge, interests and experiences. Taking responsibility for, and ownership of, one's own learning is an essential part of the whole process, but one which seems to receive little attention. Children in nursery classes are afforded great freedom and autonomy over their own learning. For instance, the

American High Scope programme designed by Weikart in the 1970s for disadvantaged inner city pre-schoolers, and now in use in some enlightened authorities here is based on this. The programme requires each child to 'Plan; do; review' their day, which is an excellent learning model. Even in the average pre-school group children may choose activities. This choice, paradoxically, is incrementally removed as a child progresses through the present educational machinery, so that by mid-secondary school no choice of what, when and where learning takes place remains to the pupil. Why? Arguments for administrative purposes should not be allowed to prevail against good educational practice.

Memory

Providing the pupil has been able to make sense of the educational experiences to the extent that they are 'owned' internally, recall should not be a serious problem. Older children, if taught study skills, will be able to check their recall for themselves through homework. Attainment tests are, currently, the last measure of this in schools. But in real life, it is what we *do* with this knowledge and information that distinguishes the fool from the successful individual. The real test of intelligent behaviour is the ability to transfer what is learned in one situation and to put it to use in another. Or, as J. S. Bruner termed it in *The Process of Education*, 'going beyond the information given'.

Meeting the individual needs of pupils

> 'The teacher's role as guide and mentor to each individual pupil . . . requires both careful monitoring and recording of pupils' progress, and an understanding of individual capacities and difficulties.'
> (*Better Schools*)

The HMI survey expressed concerned at the lack of preparation students were given in these difficult aspects of teaching. Fewer than half the courses seen were providing students with an understanding of the varieties of pupils' needs in terms of ability, culture, and background, or helping students to make their teaching relevant and interesting to the full range of pupils. There is a need to understand that the content and processes of learning have to be appropriate to the pupils' level of understanding and previous experience; that they benefit from approaching new ideas through familiar contexts, and that they need to appreciate the relevance of what they are learning to their immediate or future needs.

Grouping by ability is rarely effective if used as the sole means of mediating the curriculum for the slower learners. By far the best mediator of the curriculum is the teacher who uses different kinds of language with different pupils; varies the pace of introducing the new, and carefully judges the timing and amount of consolidation and revision which is necessary.

Curriculum areas

Numerous reports over the past decade have deplored the paucity of the curriculum offered to many children with special educational needs. Perhaps some of the poorest have been in secondary schools were uncertainty of aims, objectives and methods appeared to be the rule, and the curriculum a hotchpotch of disconnected subject teaching. The Bullock Report (1975) referred to 'a monotonous and prolonged emphasis on remedial work in basic skills'. It is to be hoped that all that is now changing, but just in case it has not, let us look at ways to engage those children with learning and behavioural difficulties in the processes of their own learning.

The centrality of the arts in the curriculum

The Warnock Report spelt out the goals of education, and laid emphasis on 'awareness of moral values and *capacity for enjoyment*', and after formal education to become 'an active participant in society and a responsible contributor to it, capable of achieving as much independence as possible'.

The Expressive Arts provide a three-fold means of achieving these goals for all children, but especially for children with SEN.

(1) For many children with little or impaired ability to communicate by traditional methods of speech, reading and writing, the Arts offer other channels of communication through movement, music or visual imagery, from which they gain immense pleasure and enrichment on what might otherwise be a limited and arid world.

(2) It is now well recognised that many children with SEN do not learn incidentally and may have great difficulty in learning by accepted academic methods. They may more easily acquire

68

concepts through direct experiences in the Arts. Take music, for instance: peoples throughout the world and throughout history have voiced their feelings, described events, given praise or lamented, and told stories through music and dance. All babies can dance and sing long before they can walk or talk.

Counting aloud in music and simple dance patterns help to reinforce shape and number concepts taught in more formal lessons. The child's whole body and thought is involved. Indeed to dance in a group requires quite sophisticated coordination of the senses of sight (not to bump into each other, to keep shapes and spaces), hearing, (to keep tempo and rhythm, and to blend with the movements of others), and a kinaesthetic, or motor, sense of where all the body parts are in space and in relation to other people.

A movement memory is also needed, and that is something we all need (to play a piano or drive a car for instance) but which is overlooked in memory training programmes in schools.

The development of language is also greatly eased and enhanced in creative activities, for words may be needed to describe a movement, a skill, a process or a meaning.

The Rudolph Steiner schools aim at a curriculum balanced between intellect and emotion, and quote Bruno Bettleheim saying 'that anything that increases the feeling of being a good, worthwhile person is curative'.

It seems to be all the more important therefore that we make just as careful plans for the social and emotional development of our children as we do for their intellectual development, and the Arts provide the obvious media. What better way of learning to listen to other people's point of view; take criticism (if given kindly and constructively); learn that you are not the hub of the universe, but that working as part of a group can be a lot more fun when involved in, say, a drama workshop or music group, or a collective art project. All gain in enjoyment and the growth of self-esteem and confidence.

For children with learning difficulties these are easier, more natural, channels of communication and learning. Music, be it singing or playing an instrument, is a motor activity and needs some degree of motor control, mental concentration and, if it is not to be a solitary activity, a degree of cooperation and turn-taking with others similarly engaged. Drama affords many similar opportunities for learning.

(3) The third value of the Arts for children with SEN is frequently overlooked.

For some the Arts prove to be their metier, and they find they are the equal, or even the superior of their 'normal' peers in terms of achievement. The value in self-worth and personal growth for these young people is immense, raising not only their own status and expectations, but, just as importantly, raising the expectations of parents and teachers. For a few their achievements receive wider public acclaim; the acclaim being based on the quality of the work and not because the creator is 'handicapped'. The works of Christy Brown, Stephen Wiltshire and Christopher Nolan in the fields of art and literature are most notable. (*The Centrality of the Arts in the Curriculum*, J. Hull)

The use of PE to identify and remediate difficulties

Primary school teachers who take their own classes for physical activities have the edge over secondary teachers since they have invaluable opportunities to observe children in action.

What is the connection between PE and SEN? A child with a reading or speech problem may also display difficulties in physical organisation. For a child to distinguish between 'b' and 'd', or 'p' and 'q' or 's' and '8' requires tiny and speedy discriminations in shape and orientation. It is something we all do a million times a day without giving it a second's conscious thought. It does take for granted, however that we 'know' what is 'front', 'back', 'up', 'down', 'left' and 'right' and can judge length and distance reasonably well. Some children, for a variety of reasons, simply cannot organise themselves in space in this way. Such children are sometimes labelled 'clumsy', and much has been written about 'the clumsy child syndrome'.

We are all of us clumsy at some time or another, and some people are better coordinated than others, but these children are continuously and consistently experiencing difficulties. It is in PE lessons that they are easiest to spot. They literally have 'two left feet', (often with their shoes reversed and shirts unevenly buttoned). They find it extremely difficult to follow verbal instructions in movement. For instance a command to run and then stop often results in 'overrunning', as though there is a time lag for the muscles to obey the brain command; or an instruction to raise the left arm can result in the child raising its right arm or even a leg! All this assumes of course that the child is not just being wilful and naughty, but experience and knowing your children soon sorts that out.

A further important aspect of PE lessons is in having a sound knowledge of child development, physical as well as intellectual, which then enables you to observe the differing rates of development and ability. In turn this enables you to plan for differing levels of activities to suit those variable growth rates. Between the ages of 9 and 14 there are tremendous differences in growth, with girls often outstripping boys in both strength, ability and intellectual development.

Science

In all science lessons consider whether what you are planning is appropriate, and ensure that what you are presenting can be tackled by all. Consider also the needs of the physically disabled and girls, and choose your examples accordingly. For instance in a topic on heat you may reach for an example from the combustion engine, when it could quite easily alternate with one from cooking. Both subjects are likely to be of interest and within the experiences of both boys and girls.

Formal assessment and the 1981 Education Act

When all help has been given, there may still be one or two children whose needs the school cannot meet. After all external help, from the educational psychologist, speech therapist, and advisory SEN teachers, has been sought, then a request can be made for a formal assessment which may lead to a Statement of Need under the 1981 Act. Under Section 1 (2), the Act deems a child to have special educational needs if he has a learning difficulty which requires special provision to meet those needs. A child has a 'learning difficulty' if:

(a) he has a significantly greater difficulty in learning than the majority of children of his age; or
(b) he suffers from a disability which either prevents or hinders him from making use of educational facilities of a kind generally provided in schools, within the area of the local authority concerned, for children of his age.

Section 1 (4) excludes a learning difficulty which arises solely because the language of instruction is different from the language of the pupil's home.

If, as a result of the full assessment a child is found to have learning difficulties under these criteria, s/he becomes the 'subject of a statement'. A statemented child should be able to be supported in a mainstream school unless the disability is so severe as to require highly specialised teaching or treatment that cannot be provided in an ordinary school. 'Support' must be defined in the statement and may range from physical aids, extra helper time (for, say toileting), to extra teaching support. The ways in which local authorities have developed policies and resources to provide this support vary enormously. Interpretation of the conditions under which children should be educated are, to some extent, governed by the funds allocated to Special Education. Educational debate rages over the desirability of special schools versus integration, but in practice, most authorities have opted for a mixed economy and retained, but expanded, the role of special schools.

Pre-course visits

It should be a pre-course requirement for students to have visited at least one special school or unit, for most have no previous experience or knowledge of children with disabilities or learning difficulties. A recurring comment from experienced teachers visiting such schools for the first time was on the high expectations and achievements of the children. Even if your course does not require this of you, I would strongly urge that you arrange such a visit for yourself in the vacation. As school terms are longer than college terms this should be perfectly possible. You may even be tempted to join in and lend a hand!

Summary

This is the longest chapter in the book because it covers areas that give most concern to all teachers, not just the inexperienced. The main points are summarised as:

- Intelligence is not immutable. It can change.
- Children with SEN account for up to 20% of the school population; that could be 5 or 6 in every mixed ability class.
- They cover a wide range of ability and disability and are not necessarily the dullest or slowest. There is no hard and fast dividing line between 'normal' and 'special'.
- The teaching of these children is the responsibility of every teacher.
- Educational failure is the result of many factors; therefore
  - (1) the earliest identification of any difficulty is essential if it is not to become compounded and chronic.
  - (2) know your children as individuals.

(3) a good knowledge of child development of an earlier age than the one you teach helps you to recognise immature learning and behaviour patterns.

● Frequent and/or intermittent absence is a major factor in the development of learning difficulties.

● There may be up to 30% of children in ordinary schools who suffer from minimal intermittent hearing loss.

● There may be gross mismatches cognitively and developmentally in children with SEN, but their needs are the same as all children's, and there are always more similarities than differences with their peers.

● Teaching should be designed to afford them genuine success through respect for their work, and praise for their efforts.

● Quality of presentation and materials is their right. Only the best is good enough. If *you* don't give them the opportunities to experience excellence, who will?

● Do not hesitate to seek further help if you feel this is needed.

No child should leave school feeling he is a failure.

'Learning is not worth a penny when joy and courage are lost along the way'   Pestalozzi

References

Brown, C. 1989. *My Left Foot* Faber and Faber.

Bruner, J. S. (1960). *The Process of Education*. Harvard.

Bullock, A. (1975). *Language for Life*. HMSO.

DES (1978). 'Special Educational Needs', *Warnock Report*. HMSO.

Education Act (1981). *Special Educational Needs*. HMSO.

DES (1985). Better Schools. HMSO.

Hull, J. (1990). 'The Centrality of the Arts in the Curriculum in *'Creative Arts and Mental Disability'*, ed. S. Segal. A. B. Academic.

Nolan, C. (1987). *Under the Eye of the Clock*. Wiedenfeld & Nicolson.

NCC (1989). *Curriculum for All*. NCC.

Stott, D. H. (1978). *Helping Children with Learning Difficulties*. Ward Lock.

Hohmann, M., Banet, B. and Weikart, D. (1979). *Young Children in Action*. High Scope.

Wiltshire, S. (1988). *Drawings*. Dent.

'The classroom is an engineered environment.'

CHAPTER 5

'You gotta accentuate the positive'

(*Bing Crosby*)

> 'The public rightly regard standards of pupil behaviour as a touchstone of the quality of the school system'. (*Better Schools*)

> The Junior School Project provides confirmation that an effective school has a positive ethos. Overall the atmosphere was more pleasant in the effective schools ...
> Both around the school and within the classroom, less emphasis on punishment and critical control, and a greater emphasis on praise and rewarding pupils, had a positive impact. Where teachers actively encouraged self control on the part of the pupils, rather than emphasising the negative aspects of their behaviour, progress and development increased. What appeared to be important was firm but fair classroom management.
>
> (*Junior School Project*)

Schools which are able to maintain high standards of behaviour usually achieve this by promoting positive, rather than punitive, policies. Their teachers set an example and attempt to maintain good relationships with each other, the pupils, and the parents. Teachers' success can also be attributed in part to their consistent encouragement of pupils' positive attitudes, behaviour and self-discipline.

Even the best school's efforts are frustrated if the pupils are bored or not gainfully occupied. Lively imaginative teaching, plus a determination to involve pupils actively in their work will go a long way to remedy this. The curriculum will offer opportunities for this, as will a more skilful match of teaching styles to pupils' skills and abilities.

The chicken and egg syndrome

Which comes first, learning difficulties or behavioural problems? Obviously a child who is unhappy, has emotional problems either at home or at school, or whose behaviour patterns are such that he cannot settle to work or allow others to do so, is not likely to be learning much. Equally, a child who has fallen behind his peers in learning, will become increasingly disenchanted with lessons where he cannot succeed, and, the devil finding mischief . . . will find other things to gain your attention! Labels such as 'disruptive', 'naughty', 'disobedient', 'maladjusted' soon become attached. Other cliches follow, and the children will live up to their reputations if they feel that is the only way they can achieve recognition. How, then, do we break into the vicious vortex of failure and opprobrium?

Before attempting an answer to that question it might be sensible to define more exactly what is meant by 'maladjusted'. The 1945 Regulations on handicapped pupils defined maladjusted children as those who 'show evidence of emotional instability or psychological disturbance and who require special educational treatment in order to effect their personal, social or educational re-adjustment'. This still seems as good a definition as any, for two reasons.

Although many children may at some time be described by exasperated teachers as 'maladjusted', when the full meanings of 'emotional instability' and 'psychological disturbance' are investigated there are very few indeed in the ordinary school to whom the term should properly be applied. For those unhappy few, specialised educational programmes are needed.

The positive message explicit in the words 'educational re-adjustment' should cheer the hard-pressed teacher. Clearly it is not considered a permanent state, and given the right conditions and teaching, the child can develop more personally and socially satisfying behaviour.

However, because they can be so exhausting and difficult to manage, and their behaviour seem so inexplicable, children with emotional and behavioural difficulties (EBD) attract the least sympathy and the least resources in the education system. Because their appearance (and behaviour for much of the time) is normal, the response they evoke is different to those children with more obvious 'handicaps'.

If maladjustment is not manifest at all times, it is obviously worth looking at the context in which it appears.

There are a number of behaviour checklists designed to identify aspects of maladjustment to school settings. Some are complicated, others lengthy. One of the easiest for the busy teacher is 'The Child at School', an observation schedule devised by ILEA to give information on children's adjustment to school. There are three subscales assessing learning difficulties, anxiety, and aggressive behaviours. It was designed for use with junior and first year secondary pupils, and is relatively quick and easy to use. It requires the teacher to make judgments based on their knowledge and experience of the child and others of the same age. As with all exercises of this kind, the whole schedule should be read through first, and then each pair of statements considered separately and in relation to the child as you know him (not other people's views of him).

The following version is arranged to give the teacher a clear picture of the child's areas of difficulty. The first three items identify predominantly learning difficulties; the second three social and anxiety problems; and the third three, aggressive behaviours.

Scoring is on a five point scale.

Tick 1 if statement A is true ALL OR MOST OF THE TIME.
Tick 2 if statement A is USUALLY TRUE.
Tick 3 if s/he is sometimes one and sometimes the other.
Tick 4 if statement B is USUALLY TRUE of the child.
Tick 5 if statement B is true MOST OF THE TIME.

STATEMENT A	1	2	3	4	5	STATEMENT B
1. Eager to learn; curious and inquiring child.						Shows little interest, curiosity or motivation in learning.
2. Can concentrate on any task. Not easily distracted.						Cannot concentrate on any particular task. Easily distracted.
3. Perseveres in the face of difficult or challenging work.						Lacks perseverance. Is impatient with difficult or challenging work.
4. A happy and contented child.						An unhappy, anxious or worried child.
5. Copes easily with new situations or people						Has difficulties in coping with new situations or people.
6. A sociable, friendly child.						Solitary, withdrawn child.
7. Even-tempered, easy-going child.						Irritable or quarrelsome child.
8. Helpful and considerate towards other children.						Bullies or is spiteful towards other children
9. Readily accepts limits, discipline and control.						Is generally disruptive, unco-operative, or disobedient.

A *low* score on each item indicates *good* adjustment and a *high* score, *poor* adjustment.

Providing you have had time to get to know the children in your class well, this should at least give you an initial indication of the aspects of a child's performance in class that need closer attention. It is, therefore, unlikely to be practicable for the student teacher, and should only be attempted by the probationer with caution.

Motivation and learning difficulties were discussed in the previous chapter. However, contrary to popular belief, it should be stressed that *all children want to learn*, despite outward appearances, and the 'hard', disinterested front is put on by many to hide their feelings of failure. They may have experienced so much failure, ridicule and criticism that they have switched off, and are now afraid of trying. This can happen at a very early age, and pupils become adept at hiding their disappointment and shame (as they see it). The tough mask of bravado is used to disparage the 'clever' ones, and dismiss as 'silly', 'boring', 'babyish' what you are trying to teach.

No child is completely incapable. What are they good at? Find out; you may be pleasantly surprised when you take the trouble to get to know them. Above all, avoid developing the 'siege mentality' of 'them' against 'me'. No-one gains from that. Having said that, *how* to motivate is a most difficult task for a teacher. Motivation has to be intrinsic; that is, it has to come from within the child. A teacher cannot motivate out of the blue, or in a vacuum. It has to be done via the momentum of success. In other words, 'nothing succeeds like success'. Constructing a series of attainable targets that clearly demonstrate successful work begins the process. The secret is to build up the momentum so that good work becomes the accepted norm. It is worth remembering that *a child who is being good can't be bad at the same time*!

Disturbed and disturbing

It is important to distinguish between 'disturbed' and 'disturbing'.

Some children are emotionally disturbed within themselves. The reasons may be for us to see, or may be deep rooted, obscure and possibly a matter for a psychologist or psychiatrist. In class they may easily be overlooked, and for this reason it is important that you are aware of their existence. They are often very quiet, withdrawn, sad, incurious children, who give no trouble, but do not achieve anything either. Stott describes this group of behaviours as 'under-reacting'.

Girls outnumber boys by about 4 to 1 in this condition. Boys tend to manifest their problems in more physical extrovert ways.

Children who are disturbing – to their teachers and those around them – cannot fail to escape your attention, for that is exactly what they seek. Their behaviour is a barrier to their own learning, and if unchecked, becomes a barrier to others'. These behaviours can be called 'over-reacting', and, unsurprisingly, boys outnumber girls by 5 to 1.

'Skill is behaviour at its best' G. P. Meredith

All children have potential and can learn through skills. Children with behavioural difficulties lack the very basic skill which we attempt to teach in infancy, *Consequences*: 'If I pinch the baby what will happen?' 'The baby screamed; Mummy was cross; I didn't get that ice cream I wanted'.

Somewhere along the line this game of consequences has not been learned. There is a failure to rehearse an action in the mind and see its consequences. The result in later life is very painful for all in the vicinity.

In many ways the 'what if?' ability in people equates well with intelligence. By questioning and seeking answers to consequences we learn a great deal about the world. It is the basis of hypothesis, and is an attribute we should be seeking to develop in our pupils. Creative children are inventive explorers, with an urge, a 'need to know', a high degree of 'effectiveness-motivation' (Stott) which is the key to learning. Paradoxically, many children with behavioural difficulties have a very highly developed sense of curiosity, the 'what if?' quality. It is precisely because of their inability to make judgments on what is sensible, practical, safe, or appropriate that their (often high) intelligence is clouded.

Behaviour modification techniques

In the past many teachers expressed outrage at the notion of manipulating children's behaviour by overt behavioural methods. But if skill is behaviour at its best, then surely that is what we are in business for? Teachers are paid to ensure that their pupils acquire a variety of skills. Such methods were criticised for being mechanistic and inapplicable to the classroom. Some of this may have been justified before teachers themselves understood the principles, and before appropriate and manageable techniques were developed. Like it or not we are all socially conditioned to respond in certain ways to stimuli in the same way that Skinner's rats did. For instance, most people respond to an outstretched hand in greeting by shaking it; most of us pick up the telephone when it rings, and so on. So, if this conditioning is so easy, universal and powerful, it is extremely shortsighted, not to say wilful, not to employ it in our own repertoire of teaching skills.

The basic premise is that all behaviour is learned. Some behaviours are anti-social, or inappropriate, and must therefore be replaced by appropriate, desirable behaviours. It is as simple as that – at least in theory! There are numerous techniques for attaining these goals; some simple, some less so. For success in any of them three things are essential:

- The underlying principles need to be thoroughly understood beforehand
- The teacher must know her pupil well
- The technique must be used consistently until the changed behaviour is firmly established

To ignore any of these three points will result in failure. For this reason it is not a suitable technique for use by student teachers or probationers at the beginning of their first teaching year. Nevertheless, and for future reference, a simplified outline of the principles follow. As you gain in knowledge and confidence, you will want to use the simpler ones.

The ABC of behaviour

Behaviours occur in a context, a setting. They must therefore be examined in context; shouting encouragement, for instance, is fine at a football match, but not in a classroom. Skinner, the pioneer psychologist in this field, said that a person has a problem when he is unable to make an appropriate response in a particular situation.

In order to identify specific problem behaviours it is necessary first to know what triggers them off; the events immediately before the behaviour occurs; the *Antecedents*. B is for the *Background* in which the *Behaviour* occurred. C is the *Consequence* of that behaviour.

ANTECEDENTS ---〉 BEHAVIOUR ---〉 CONSEQUENCES
A   B   C

The next step is to identify the behaviour, and describe it clearly. In order to do this it is necessary to eliminate what Mager in 'Goal Analysis', quoted by Westmacott and Cameron, calls 'fuzzies'. These are unclear, often subjective descriptions that don't help the design of suitable strategies. They are often met in teachers' reports! What is needed are accurate descriptions of *performance*. Phrases such as 'He can't sit still' are better described as 'He can only sit at a task for three minutes'. Or, 'She is very aggressive', meaning 'If another child takes a toy she is playing with, she bites.' Knowledge of child development is essential, for this sort of behaviour is not uncommon in two-year-olds, but would be considered bizarre in a seven-year-old.

> Translating fuzzies into performances enables all involved to pinpoint problem behaviour. Fortunately it is a relatively easy task... All the enquirer has to say is 'Exactly what would I see happening when Fred was being (insert fuzzy of your choice)?'

This quotation is from Westmacott and Cameron's excellent and amusing book on behaviour modification in the classroom, *Behaviour Can Change*. They go on to point out that 'fuzzies' are usually verbs, and ask how you would observe a child 'believing', 'understanding', 'being aware of'. Add an adverb like 'really' or 'interestingly', and they claim it is a certain fuzzy. Verbs open to fewer interpretations, and therefore more clearly describing a behaviour are: to write, to name, to select, and so on.

Having identified and described the behaviours accurately, the next stage is to create a *Priority Problem List* (PPL). This consists of:

● Listing assets; positive comments about good behaviours
● Listing deficits; describing problem behaviours
● An agreed priority problem; (you can't tackle them all at once. Pick the most immediate)
● State the desired outcome. These must be attainable in a realistic time scale

Strategies for changing A, B or C

Once the antecedents of undesirable behaviour have been identified, it is often quite simple to anticipate and sidestep them. For instance, a child who 'creates a scene', throws a tantrum, or refuses to clear away at the end of a session, will be helped by any or all of the following (as will the whole class).

Early Warning Systems Give a reminder that in five minutes it will be time to clear away, so they should finish what they are doing. A further two minute warning may be necessary for the child with a problem. No-one likes to be torn away from something they are engrossed in, or have nearly finished, so be fair.

Sugaring the Pill Wrapping a small reward around an unpleasant task; 'Once all the paint pots and brushes are clean, we can have a story'. Take care this does not develop into bribery. Children are very quick to spot that opportunity, and have no qualms about manipulating *your* behaviour!

Removing Temptation An easy one where it is possible. Just as you will not leave chocolate biscuits in view if you are on a diet, do not leave potential trouble triggers around. If you have a child who flicks paper pellets or erasers, do not hand out rulers until they are needed.

Taking Avoiding Action Where you can see potential trouble such as a tantrum, building up, a quick diversion can work wonders, especially with young children. Distracting their attention abruptly from the source of trouble seems to break the emotional tension, if followed by an alternative activity. 'Oh, look at that bird. What is he doing? What colour is his beak . . .'

Do I make myself Clear? Giving clear unambiguous instructions so that there are no excuses for misunderstandings pre-empts many potential danger spots. Procedures for entry and exit, dinner queues, stowage of coats and bags, are some of the commonest.

Prompts A system of reminders that can be silent body language, or a short phrase that is known and agreed with your group should be helpful in general regulation of behaviour and noise levels.

Playing consequences

All behaviours are learned; all behaviours have consequences. It follows, therefore, that for the child with problem behaviours the consequences must be rewarding for the behaviours to persist. These rewards can be material – sweets, watching television, 'getting their own way', exerting power over adults, sometimes to the point of emotional blackmail. Or they can result in attention from powerful adults – teachers and parents. 'Attention is to a child as sunshine is to a flower' (Westmacott and Cameron). It would seem logical, therefore, to attempt to change undesirable behaviours by reversing the expected consequences.

We all crave and need attention. The child who has been unable to gain it by approved methods (academic achievement, social skills) resorts to strong arm tactics of misbehaviour. Success is sometimes of satisfyingly monumental proportions in terms of adult reaction! So, instead of being manipulated, we must manipulate. The child needs and deserves attention. How much, and for what is for you to determine.

Selective attention means giving attention in the form of approval, when the child is doing what we want, and *not* giving it when he is not, although, clearly, dangerous or disruptive behaviours cannot be ignored. Approval should be regulated and not overdone. Children are very quick to spot the insincere and spurious, so praise that is disproportionate quickly loses currency and becomes counter-productive. Approval need not be verbal. It can be a smile, a small gesture, a wink, or even a slight pat on the shoulder. Larger reinforcers can then be given with comments such as 'I'm so pleased to see that you've been sitting working at your maths for the past ten minutes', which indicates that you have been noticing, but at the same time ignoring the times when he was not in his seat. The golden rule is *never use a bigger reinforcer than necessary*.

Contracts

With all but the youngest children contracts can be very powerful motivators in changing behaviours. They can be of the simple, informal kind that results from a quiet talk after school along the lines of 'This really can't continue, can it? What are we doing to do about it?' Then follows a discussion of the identified problem and its consequences, possible strategies for change, an agreed 'bargain' with a realistic built-in time scale, and a reward. 'Let's see if you can keep your hands to yourself for the rest of today, and then I'll find you that book on cars that you wanted'.

More formal written contracts with older children are very effective and can also involve parents in behaviours that concern both school and home. Completion of homework versus watching television is a case in point. A clear statement of what is to be done, when and where, and the outcome, is signed by all parties concerned. Interestingly, this approach usually means that the adults also have to change their behaviour to some extent, even if only to acknowledge good behaviour!

It should be clear from this brief outline of behaviour modification techniques that they are eminently suitable for changing disorders of conduct, but would be of little help to a child with more emotional difficulties.

Therapeutic activities

In *Maladjusted Children in the Ordinary School* Laslett points out the therapeutic qualities of exposure to well written or well told stories. 'In extracts from biographies . . . maladjusted children can discover how others manage in circumstances similar to their own. And literature, especially poetry, is to do with feelings, and their expression in poignant, humorous or stirring language'.

Being read aloud to at any age is a pleasure. Think of the continuing popularity of 'Book at Bedtime'. I can never understand why, in schools, it is considered suitable only for the youngest children. For reluctant readers and children with learning difficulties it is especially valuable, providing a good adult model of fluency evoking pleasure and excitement. Many children are not witness to the phenomena of adults enjoying a good read. There should be time set aside in every school every day for a short period of reading. At least one secondary school does this for fifteen minutes at the beginning of each afternoon session. It settles the whole school to work, and can take any form; silent individual reading by teachers and pupils; remedial sessions for some; reading aloud or being read aloud to for others.

It has long been known that our moods can be affected by music. A young man preparing an evening at home will greet his lover with 'soft lights and sweet music'; supermarkets play middle of the road slow 'musak' to make you relax, feel expansive and linger, changing it to something brisker shortly before closing time to hurry you out. Music could be used by schools in the same way. Supposing you take a class for art where you want the children to be calm and reflective, but they have just come from a PE lesson. They are bound to bring with them the mood of the previous lesson which you need to disperse and replace with what you want as a working atmosphere *as quickly as possible*. A tape recorder playing quietly as they enter the room works wonders, and you can create whatever mood is appropriate for the lesson. Quiet background music can also be a help when pupils are working quietly on their own creations in a particular lesson.

Sanctions

> 'Make the punishment fit the crime . . .'   (Gilbert and Sullivan)

There is no evidence that punishment results in long term improved behaviour.

> 'Schools which employ a range of rewards can use withdrawal of privileges as a sanction. This can be particularly effective if it is seen to match the offence, and if pupils themselves are drawn into the discussion.'   (HMI, *Education Observed*)

There is a clear distinction between punishment, which is actively imposed and is not part of normal life, and sanctions which are seen as part of a just system where privileges are awarded or withdrawn according to the degree of responsibility accepted and demonstrated by the pupils. Power is added to this form of control where it is made clear that it is the miscreant's beheaviour that is disapproved of by their peers as well as the teachers. Disapproval must always be confined to the *behaviour* and must not extend to the whole person. Character assassination is unforgivably cruel and can do the most far reaching damage.

For the student or new teacher life will obviously be less stressful in a school which operates a clear and consistently maintained system of rewards and sanctions. It is then easy to compile your own system to cope with minor misdemeanours, knowing that a back-up system exists in the school for more serious offences. Where an offence has been committed, it is important for the child to understand why what they have done is disapproved of, and how they can put it right, or ensure it does not happen again. Detention after school, a common practice in some schools, should be used with caution. Parents must be notified if the child will arrive home late; school transport may be an issue; specific tasks relevant to class work, or missed homework are better than time wasting 'lines'.

Although it is sometimes difficult to discover a particular culprit, *never* keep a whole group in as a punishment. It is the quickest destroyer of good class relationship, for you alienate all the innocents who will be full of righteous indignation.

'Making the punishment fit the crime' is often possible, when mess and damage have resulted. Picking up litter and general clearing up are both useful and salutary, as well as encouraging the principle of respect for one's environment.

The Elton Report, 1989

A committee chaired by Lord Elton, under pressure from all sections of the populace, looked at the problems of violence and indiscipline in schools. They concluded that counselling and guidance were neglected as classroom management techniques on most teacher education courses. They also concluded that a few LEAs have policies for supporting teachers experiencing difficulty in class control, or in managing difficult pupils, and that Inset opportunities were very limited.

They noted that on the whole teachers do not seek help in this area because it is seen as professional failure. Some see their classes as hostile, and create a negative atmosphere by carping criticism, and very rare praise, which in turn soon leads to confrontations – a dangerous downward spiral. Sarcasm is referred to as the lowest form of discipline. More older boys than girls become disaffected with school, and the recommendation is to remotivate them for learning by recognition of their non-academic achievements in records of achievement. It seems that primary school teachers do not have to cope so much with aggression directed at them, as with physical aggression between pupils.

Other recommendations are:

● Racial harassment by pupils or staff should be a disciplinary offence
● There should be a whole school policy on discipline which is clearly understood by all
● The school should strike a healthy balance between rewards and punishment, both of which should be clearly understood
● Punishment of whole groups and punishment which humiliates should be avoided
● Teachers should be alert to signs of bullying and racial harassment
● There should be mutual support amongst staff, and backing from the school
● Parents should be urged to take greater direct responsibility for their children's behaviour.

Bullying is far more common in schools than would appear at first glance. It would appear that less than half the children who are regularly bullied ever report it either to teachers or parents. This makes it doubly difficult to detect in schools, but areas of the school that afford opportunities should be well patrolled.

Clearly, a whole school policy on discipline will ease your introduction to teaching considerably. It should by now be obvious to you that as many problems are school created or school related as are child created. If you find yourself in a less than perfect school, you cannot change the system single handed, but you can legitimately ask for, and expect reasonable support in 'law enforcement'.

You will by now have detected a great deal of the hidden curriculum in this chapter. In his article, 'A New Perspective on Behavioural Problems in Schools', G. Upton dubs this 'an ecosystemic approach' in an article purporting to launch yet another system for dealing with problem behaviours. Essentially it at last acknowledges that the difficulties many children present are not entirely of their own making, but may owe much to the personality or presentation of the teacher, or be due to the inappropriateness of the school regime; what in fact I have long called 'school created, or school related problems' engendered within the school system itself. The ecosystemic approach takes the holistic view of the child and his behaviour in the context of all concerned and contributing parties, teachers as well as parents; exactly as outlined here.

Summary

- Be eclectic and flexible in your approach to 'discipline'. The key to success is to know your pupils as individuals, and then decide on the best approach to fit the situation.
- All the strategies suggested involve two factors:
  (1) Negotiation and open agreement between pupil and teacher.
  (2) As far as possible handing responsibility to the child for their behaviour (as with learning).
- *In every lesson praise should outnumber censure.* This will be difficult at first until it becomes second nature, and at times seem an impossibility. Don't be discouraged, however. It does work, and has been proved on the battlefield of the classroom.
- You will note that there are no punishments suggested. Punishment is counter productive. It does not replace bad behaviour by good; it alienates the punished and destroys relationships; it is ineffective in changing behaviour.

Lastly, don't try all these ideas at once. Decide what is easiest for you to achieve and do that first. Decide what is *your* priority – maybe to reduce the general noise level in the class, or to anchor Gary to his seat for more than ten seconds? Think about a strategy or devise an intervention and its possible outcomes. Above all, keep a sense of humour.

References

HMI (1987). *Education Observed 5*. DES.
HMI (1989). 'Discipline in Schools' (*Elton Report*). HMSO.
ILEA (1986). *The Junior School Project*. ILEA.
Laslett, R. (1982). *Maladjusted Children in the Ordinary School*. NCSE.
Stott, D. H. (1978). *Helping the Maladjusted Child*. OU.
Upton, G. (1990). 'A New Perspective on Behavioural Problems in Schools', in *MATE* Vol 8, No 1. AWMC.
Weber, K. (1982). *The Teacher is the Key*. OU.
Westmacott, E. and Cameron, R. J. (1981). *Behaviour Can Change*. Globe.
Wolfendale, S. and Bryans, T. (1989). *Managing Behaviour*. NARE.

'*Records should be brief, accessible, cumulative and up-to-date.*'

CHAPTER 6

Keeping Tabs

Teaching, learning and assessment are inter-related. Assessment should form a natural part of teaching and learning activities.
(A Guide to Assessment, SEAC, 1990)

Too often the assessment tail wags the educational dog.
(Assessing Students. How Shall We Know Them? by D. Rowntree)

This chapter is about assessment and record keeping. The two are inextricably linked. If an assessment of a pupil's work and progress is required, then there must be records to refer to, to support and evaluate it. Or, to start from the other end, what is the point of keeping records if they do not contribute to assessment?

You will be aware of the tide of protest and criticism that resulted from the earliest proposals for assessment on a national scale. Teachers, especially those in primary schools, were quick to point out that if they were to meet all the test targets there would be no time for teaching. This is an inherent danger in assessment, so it is important for you to be absolutely clear *why*, *how*, and *what* you are assessing and recording. *Time* is the most precious commodity for both teacher and child. Childhood is brief, so time which could be spent in profitable learning must not be wasted. *Therefore, assessment must be specific and effective, and recording must be brief and useful.*

The full benefits of a good recording and assessment system are only realised when they are linked to curriculum planning. They are central to a problem-solving approach to teaching. What has been described as an 'assessment through teaching' model is most applicable to young children and those with learning, behavioural and physical difficulties, but has equal relevance to older pupils. (Hull, Powell and Cooper, 1989). Realisation of the power of this teaching model is evident in the Report published in 1988 by the Task Group on Assessment and

Teaching (TGAT), in which fears expressed as to the effects of assessment on pupils are allayed by reference to the graded assessment schemes from which teachers and pupils reported enhanced motivation through up-to-date knowledge of targets and progress. Much under achievement is the result of poor self-concepts and low expectation by both pupil and teacher.

Given the present plethora of documents on both subjects, many teachers find themselves bewildered and bemused by apparently conflicting demands on their time and energies. It would seem sensible, therefore, to start from first principles and ask the naive but necessary questions of both assessment and recording:

> *Why?* Why do we need to assess children and their work?
> Why do we need to keep records?

and

> *How* How do we assess children and their work?
> How do we keep sensible records?

The function and purposes of assessment

The easiest way to answer the why and how questions, and throw in the occasional what to . . . ? is best presented in the opposite diagram.

The top half of the diagram answers most of the why questions; the bottom half the how questions.

The *purposes* of assessment are two-fold. They can be either diagnostic/prescriptive (that is *formative*), or measure *attainment* (that is *summative*).

The *methods* available can be *formal* (fulfilling some of the attainment objectives, and may be summative), or *informal*, using a range of tools from checklists, objective tests, observations or self-assessments.

Both formal and informal methods can be combined to build a *profile* of the whole pupil, as in a school leaver's record of achievement, or a particular aspect of learning, for instance the Aston Index's profile of language skills in the younger child.

Diagnostic and prescriptive assessments

Evaluation for diagnostic purposes is a relatively new practice in mainstream education, although it has long been a central part of special education.

The Purpose and Function of Assessment

W
H
Y

Assessment

PURPOSE

Diagnostic/Prescriptive

1. To determine ability/disability.
2. To determine potential
3. To indicate teaching programme.
4. To assess personality traits.
   (aptitudes & attitudes)

Attainment

1. To establish present levels of functioning.
2. To evaluate present knowledge of a subject.
3. To assess progress (relative to peers or self).
4. To build a profile of the whole person.
5. To indicate future placement in class or employment.
6. To award qualification from a recognised body.

H
O
W

METHODS

Informal

1. Checklists.
2. Objective Tests.
3. Observations.
4. Self-assessment.

Profiles

Formal

1. Examinations
   (pass/fail—grades)
2. Standardised Tests
   (NFER, SATs)
3. Continuous Assessment.

These assessments are the ones most closely linked to a problem solving approach to teaching, where by establishing levels of ability or difficulties, future teaching programmes, (or interventions in the case of behavioural difficulties) can be planned. One such is contained in 'Assessment and Record Keeping in the Mainstream School' by J. Hull, E. Powell and L. Cooper published in 1989. This is a response to schools' recognition that early identification of children with special educational needs and speedy intervention can prevent the development of chronic, long-term difficulties. It is a set of simple recording strategies that can be used and kept up-to-date by a busy class teacher. The assessment is integral to a recording system, and, in turn, informs the school and parent as to what should be the next step. Just as importantly, it records the outcome of the previous step, so forming an effective feedback loop of evaluation. The essence of the system is that records should be *brief, accesssible, cumulative and up-to-date.* In that way a system is manageable, is integral to any other system operating in the school, and goes with the child to the next teacher, class, or school.

The TGAT report supports this by stressing that both formative and summative forms of assessment must 'both feed back to the pupil and feed forward to the next teacher or institution'. It emphasises the 'feed forward' aspects of formative assessment with its 'implications that the teacher responsible for making the assessments will not be those responsible for acting upon them'. This is an important point to remember.

Attainment

This is the area of assessment most familiar to teachers. It includes tests to establish the present level of functioning, as in intelligence tests, although these are now not afforded their previous high status in determining children's placement in selective or special schools because of doubts as to their cultural bias. Evaluation of knowledge provides information on how much of what has been taught has been learned. This may be by a number of methods described later. A further, but distinct, use of assessment is to discover what progress (or regress) has been made, either by the individual pupil, or by the group as a whole, and to compare the progress of the individual with that of the group. From such a series of assessments a profile of ability, aptitude and attainment may be constructed, which can then be used in determining the future direction or placement of the pupil.

Finally, and this is one that you will have been recently concerned with, there is the public award of a qualification which recognises that knowledge and standards have been acquired, and which in turn offers access to particular fields of employment.

Formal methods of assessment

Besides the time honoured *examinations* consisting of set papers completed against the clock, with results expressed on a pass/fail scale, there are a number of variations for formally assessing both knowledge and skill. The General Certificate of Secondary Education now incorporates continuously assessed work, and negotiated projects between teacher and pupil alongside traditionally examined knowledge. With the introduction of the new curriculum the single examination is no longer adequate to assess certain aspects of learning and maturity. A similar difficulty arises in the assessment of the Arts. How is it possible to measure quantitatively what is essentially qualitative in knowledge, critical appreciation and judgement? Indeed the TGAT report specifically recommends 'that assessment of attitudes should not form a prescribed part of the national assessment system'.

The difficulties inherent in attempting to impose a single system of standards across all disciplines is highlighted in the classic division between the sciences and humanities. Science has been defined as an attempt to arrive at a consensus on phenomena of the natural world, whereas in philosophy, humanities and the arts it is proper and acceptable to differ and disagree. The educational implications are clear. How can you apply scientific methods of measurement to assess creativity, artistic potential and achievement?

Standardised tests

These are so called because they have been standardised in trials on a large population of children. They are described as 'normative tests' in that they measure what the 'normal' child at a particular age should be expected to achieve. As discussed earlier, these have been criticised, mainly on grounds of cultural bias. For instance, if the population on which the tests were standardised were predominantly white, small town, southern English children of some ten or fifteen years ago, there are a number of reasons for suspecting their validity for a mixed race, working class inner city population in the 1990s. Nevertheless, this is not to say that such tests do not have their uses.

Standardised achievement tests measure the common objectives of a wider variety of schools, and they complement rather than replace teachers' informal classroom tests.

They are especially useful for measuring general educational development, determining pupil progress from one year to the next, grouping pupils, diagnosing learning difficulties and comparing achievement with aptitude. They are of little value for measuring learning outcomes unique to a particular course, the day to day progress of pupils and knowledge of current developments in rapidly changing fields. These latter purposes are more effectively served by informal classroom tests.

(N. E. Gronlund, *Measurement and Evaluation in Teaching*)

Tests you may encounter in this category are standardised reading, maths and other tests such as those devised by the NFER. Under the national assessment system, Standard Attainment Tests (SATs) are applicable to all children in schools and will cover all subject areas.

It should be remembered that these tests are indicators of the *present* level of achievement of a pupil, and are not predictors of *future* performance of achievement. In their paper 'Able to Learn' S. Hegarty and D. Lucas found that assessment of learning ability is a better predictor of later school achievement than an intelligence test which measures only previous learning and present ability. One such test of learning ability and attitude is Stott's *Guide to a Child's Learning Skills* described in chapter 4.

Continuous assessment

This is becoming increasingly popular at all levels of education. You will probably have encountered some forms of it on your own training courses. It can be one of the most rigorous forms of assessment if carefully compiled. It offers great flexibility to suit not only the subject matter, but the assessor and assessee. Again, if it is to be professionally objective, careful records of facts and achievement are essential. Continuous assessment helps the pupil to recognise his or her own strengths and weaknesses. 'Pupils can notice their faults before being told about them by the teacher', said one sixth former, who added, 'the process helps you realise who you are'.

Informal assessment methods

Checklists

If well constructed, these can provide a good method of evaluating both knowledge and skills. In essence they are rather like a shopping list; a list of things to be acquired. They can be *developmental* in the sense that they list hierarchically the skills you would expect a child to develop in a chronological sequence. A good example of this type would be a language acquisition checklist, which would start with random sounds and progress through babble, phonemes, jargon, two word utterances, simple sentences to an understanding and use of complex sentence structures, grammar and syntax.

Criterion referenced

These tests also serve useful purposes. These may be used to check the acquisition of a set of distinct skills such as those to be found in social and personal education programmes. It may or may not be possible to arrange these skills into some sort of developmental order, but more than likely it is easier to list them as discrete skills and check them off as they are manifested in performance.

Basically a series of tasks is listed, and a tick made against each one as the skill is acquired. It may be useful to use a three point scale of 'always', 'sometimes', 'never', to indicate an intermediate stage of 'working on it but not yet there'.

The value of criterion referenced testing is that the child is not competing with his peers, but only with his own previous performance and progress. On this score they are of particular value with children for whom comparison with peers would be detrimental.

Objective tests

There has been much understandable concern about the time taken up by all the testing demands on teachers. One very effective way to cut down on the time factor is to use a set of objective tests. They are the quickest way of probing the actual acquisition of facts and knowledge, and, if well constructed, can also demand deduction and inference from the pupils. Once the principles of their construction are understood, they can be used for any age group and for any subject area.

Objective tests are constructed on a series of questions which require the pupil to respond in one of three ways. The basic rule is that the question and answer must form a grammatical whole.

The three types of question are:

(1) *Recall* A statement is made which is completed by a word, phrase, date or figure. For example:
A pig is an . . . .

(2) *Multiple Choice* The sentence is completed by making a choice from a selection of answers offered. For example:

A pig is (an animal/a fruit/a machine)

(3) *True or False* A complete statement is offered which has to be judged by ticking or ringing the correct box. For example:

A pig is a machine. T/F

From these simplistic examples it can be seen that the advantages are:

(1) Specific areas of learning can quickly be tested for assimilation of facts.

(2) For children who find writing either physically or intellectually difficult, the opportunity to demonstrate their knowledge in this easy answer format is too good to be missed.

(3) The all-important 'knowledge of results' for the pupil is immediately available if the tests are marked by the group as soon as completed as a class exercise, which then reinforces correct learning and corrects faulty answers. If everyone marks their neighbour's paper, then all are involved in a continuous group learning process. We must all recall the agony of waiting weeks for exam results, or alternatively, total indifference at the later date because we had completely forgotten what it was all about. Certainly neither experience was an active learning process.

(4) The bonus to teachers of a class marking system are obvious. You are not burning the midnight oil marking endless illegible papers!

The disadvantages are few but also obvious:

(1) The method can be used only to test undisputed factual areas.

(2) The construction of the questions can be quite time consuming, requiring careful thought to fit them into the format, but this is offset by collecting them into a bank for further use, and by the fact that no time is spent on marking.

Observation

Observation is the oldest form of assessment and it is also the form most open to criticism on the grounds of bias and subjectivity. It therefore behoves the teacher to acquire professional observational techniques, some of which have already been described. One of the cardinal rules is not to try to observe all the children all the time, but to concentrate either on one or two aspects to observe for the whole group, or to concentrate on one child at a time. For very young or handicapped children this is the area of assessment where parental contributions are invaluable; for who knows a child better than the parent or carer who is most closely involved with it for the majority of the time?

'An open policy about sharing information in the records . . . is likely to be the most effective way for the school to work in partnership with parents'. (*Assessment and Record Keeping for SEN in Mainstream Schools*)

It should perhaps be noted here that all assessment information on a child is to be treated as confidential and available only on a 'need to know' basis. The main purpose of assessment by observation is to allow the teacher to utilise his or her professional knowledge of the pupil to complement the standard forms of assessment.

Self-assessment

It may seem extravagant to make the claim that children as young as four are capable of making realistic assessments of their own capabilities and work. It is nevertheless true if systems such as 'High Scope', (with its plan-do-review formula) and the systematic and cooperative learning approach of the Coverdale system are examined. Here children are involved in the planning and management of their own learning activities. An integral part of these systems is the evaluation loop, where outcomes of the activities are reviewed by the children themselves in order to plan the next phase. These methods are simply sound management principles where better performance results when everybody is kept aware of common objectives and is involved in planning.

With older children it is possible to involve them in more subjective and sophisticated forms of self-evaluation. Selection of their own 'best work' to be included in a profile folder is one example.

A number of self-assessment forms have been devised whereby children comment on various aspects of their lives. Some are designed to develop self-concepts; others enable schools to review their own practices. A particularly useful one is where the new intake at secondary transfer are asked for their views on a range of issues after a week or so in the new school. The sorts of issues raised often focus on what the children see as four main areas of concern.

These are:

- possessions; where to keep them safely and have access to them between lessons
- lavatories; their unsavoury state and their potential for danger
- friends; access to them at break times; opportunities for socialising other than in bleak playgounds. Graffiti, smoking and misbehaviour increase when pupils are locked out of school premises
- not knowing where they should be, or who their teachers are

This can prove a highly effective agent of change in a school!

Peer tutoring is a valuable, yet grossly underused, source of learning. It probably works best in the acquisition of basic skills such as reading and mathematics. Here the child who is a stage or two ahead of a contemporary acts as tutor. The benefits to both children can be enormous. Think of your own recent efforts to acquire a new skill (say golf or wind surfing). When you have reached a new level you want to demonstrate it. Why not tap into this psychological need by using a child who has just acquired reading skills above the levels of some of her peers to work for short periods with one who needs a little help? Who better to understand any difficulties there may be than someone who has recently mastered the same steps? Everyone benefits; the child who needs help gets it more frequently than the teacher could give; the other child gets the opportunity to rehearse and reinforce newly learned skills, and, not least, the teacher is helped by the knowledge that more children are being helped. Both children can then be involved in a negotiated assessment of progress at a simple level.

How does all this fit into the new regulations for national assessment and testing?

The 1988 TGAT Report states that

> Any system of assessment should satisfy certain general criteria. For the purposes of the national assessment we give priority to the following four criteria:
>
> - the assessment results should give direct information about pupils' achievement in relation to objectives: they should be *criterion referenced*;
> - the results should provide a basis for decisions about pupils' further learning needs: they should be *formative*;
> - the scales or grades should be capable of comparison across classes and schools, if teachers, pupils and parents are to share a common

language and common standards: so the assessments should be calibrated or *moderated*;

- the ways in which criteria and scales are set up and used should relate to expected routes of educational development, giving some continuity to a pupil's assessment at different ages: the assessments should relate to *progression*.

Given these four excellent guidelines, one is led to the recommendation that the final assessment at age 16 should be *summative*.

This approach leads to the formation of a profile on the child which displays the many facets of their personality, interests, and behaviour, as well as their physical and emotional progress and intellectual attainments.

Profiles of achievement

The notion of profiling began in the early 1960s in the field of mental subnormality with Gunzberg's *Progress Assessment Charts*. These presented in pie-chart sectors all aspects of intellectual and social functioning that were felt to be capable of development in adults in a hospital for the mentally subnormal. It was a sound model which lent itself to adaptation in other fields. The Mansell report of 1979 *Basis for Choice* looked at prospects for non-examination school leavers. It recommended that profiles of all pupils should be compiled in their last two years at school to act as a basis for leaving reports and careers advice.

ILEA was probably the first to develop such a system in their London Record of Achievement (ROA). Others have since been developed. The London system builds a portfolio of pupils' work throughout secondary school, based on external examinations and graded tests. These are used in a formative way to determine courses and levels. The final profile provides a summative statement of a pupil's achievements, and records progress both within and outside the classroom, including experiences and attainments which may reflect qualities not easily discernible by examinations. For the less academic but nonetheless talented and able student, this is of paramount importance, for it is often the non-academic abilities that employers value.

The TGAT Report suggests that ROAs should begin with a summary of pupils' experience at the end of primary education. Key stage 2 assessments could form the basis of them, but they would also benefit from being set in a wider context of total experiences. If a cumulative system of record keeping has been adopted by the primary school, this should not be a daunting task.

What are the essential ingredients of profiles?

They should:

- Recognise a wide range of achievement both within and outside the curriculum
- Define and make explicit the criteria on which assessment is to be based
- Focus on success rather than failure
- Emphasise process as well as outcome
- Actively involve pupils in the planning and assessment of their learning
- Encourage the involvement of parents in reviewing and planning pupils' work

A frequent criticism against ROAs is that they are too cumbersome, and no busy employer has the time, inclination or need to read through a big portfolio of records and work. This is true, but need not present a hurdle. The summary documents can be reduced to a couple of pages which list courses taken, grades attained, and all other relevant areas of experience and achievement. It used to be the view of many employers that ROAs were irrelevant and they were only interested in exam grades. This is changing fast as they find themselves competing for a diminishing pool of school leavers. There is a growing recognition of the usefulness of a wider bank of information. 'We use the records to draw the interviewee out', said one employer. Perhaps the biggest advantage of ROAs is for the great majority of pupils who are not academic high flyers, but who will be the mainstay of the workforce.

Pupils with special educational needs

Pupils with quite severe special educational needs can also be realistically assessed and leave with a good record of achievement at the end of their school lives.

TVEI and CPVE courses are both highly suitable vehicles for leavers' programmes for most pupils with SEN. There have been a number of very successful pilot schemes for this section of the school population which previously had no authenticated recognition of their many, and often considerable, experiences, qualities and achievements.

However there are concerns that the regulations relating to the national curriculum and its assessment procedures could further disadvantage such pupils. Circular 5/89, which gives regulations for the implementation of the national curriculum and its assessment, indicates that for children statemented under the 1981 Act, the national curriculum (and therefore its assessment) may be 'disapplied' or 'modified'. There is some justification for the fears expressed that some schools would 'disapply' such children whom they regard as being expensive in resource terms, and at the same time depressing the grades of the school overall. Some safeguards to avoid this are emerging, but teachers will need to be vigilant to ensure that *all* pupils receive their entitlement to a full and broad curriculum. The SEAC's advice to the DES 'is based on the entitlement of all pupils to the full National Curriculum, which includes opportunities to be assessed. These assessments should seek to determine children's knowledge, understanding and skill in whatever way they are able to demonstrate it'.

Record keeping

Regular record-keeping provides encouragement and reassurance to parents, teachers and pupils.

> Records kept by the teacher, and regularly completed as an intrinsic part of the teaching process, are the most economical way to obtain cumulative information, and what has helped him or her learn most effectively within the classroom. These records also provide a sound basis on which to share information about a child between the child, teachers, parents and other involved professionals.
>
> Well completed records should be brief, clear, factual up-to-date and reliable, and are at the very heart of on-going assessment through teaching. (*Assessment and Record Keeping for SEN in Mainstream Schools*)

If you are clear about the purposes of the records you are keeping, then their compilation will be much easier. There is absolutely no sense in keeping records if they are not to be put to use in formulating further plans of action and/or passed on to others for information and their action. The following diagram shows the connections between the records kept by the class teacher and those of the whole school.

Each one feeds the next and no re-writing is necessary, nor do contradictions and mismatches occur.

> Teacher's daily log/diary→Individual child's record→Class summary lists→Whole school lists.

Use of a simple system like this should save you a lot of time.

Report writing

To write meaningful reports on pupils can be an extraordinarily difficult task if one is to avoid the trite clichés of the 'could do better' kind. How do you clearly and briefly summarise your knowledge and the work of each child? What is needed is a framework of reference in which to display their achievements. The word 'achievement' has been used in this chapter, so it might be useful to look at one Education Authority's definition of achievement, which, although written with secondary age pupils in mind, is perfectly applicable to any age.

Aspects of achievement

Aspect 1
This is strongly represented in the public examination system. It requires the capacity to express oneself in a written form; to retain propositional knowledge; to select quickly and appropriately from it, and to memorise and organise material.

Aspect 2
This is concerned with the practical applications of knowledge. Oral skills, problem-solving and investigational skills are more important than the retention of knowledge. It tends to be more difficult, expensive and time-consuming to assess.

Aspect 3
This is concerned with personal and social skills; the capacity to communicate and cooperate with others; initiative, self-reliance and the ability to work alone as well as with others, and the qualities of leadership. This aspect was, until recently, virtually untapped by existing examination systems.

Aspect 4
This involves motivation and commitment; the willingness to accept failure without destructive consequences; perseverance and the self-confidence to learn even difficult tasks.

Such motivation is often regarded as a prerequisite to achievement, but it can be regarded as an achievement in its own right. In one sense

aspect 4 is the most important of all, since without it other achievement either at school or in the future is likely to be very limited.
(ILEA, 'Improving Secondary Schools' from *The Hargreaves Report*)

It takes little imagination to see that these aspects are common to achievement at all ages, and could be used as a basis for assessment for younger children's reports also.

Summary

(1) Time is the most precious commodity for both teacher and pupil
(2) Be absolutely clear Why? How? What? you are assessing and recording
(3) Assessment must be specific and effective
(4) Assessment, record keeping and curriculum planning are inextricably linked
(5) Assessment should be through teaching
(6) Good assessment procedures enhance pupil motivation attainment and attendance
(7) Good assessment and record keeping procedures give a *structured freedom* for teachers to teach creatively
(8) Formative assessment focuses on the individual child's progress
(9) Records of achievement are of particular importance at secondary transfer to prevent
  (a) time wasted on repeat teaching of ground already covered, and
  (b) regress due to loss of impetus and motivation and at school leaving to provide a summative record to use for entry to further courses or employment.
(10) Assessments and records should feed forward as well as back
(11) Records should be brief, accessible, cumulative and up-to-date

New teachers should read this chapter carefully, absorb the principles expounded on the purposes and methods of assessment and record keeping, and only then *select what is most appropriate for your needs now. Don't try to do it all at once.*

References

'Task Group on Assessment and Testing' (1988). *Report*. DES.
'The ERA 88. School Curriculum and Assessment'. *Circular 5/89*. DES.
Gronlund, N. E. (1965). *Measurement and Evaluation in Teaching*. Macmillan.

106

Gunzberg, (1963). *Progress Assessment Charts.*

Hegarty, S. and Lucas, D. (1978). *Able to Learn.* NFER.

Hull, J., Powell, E. and Cooper, L. (1989). *Assessment and Record Keeping for SEN in Mainstream Schools.* Hull Associates.

ILEA (1984). 'Improving Secondary Schools' from the *Hargreaves Report.* ILEA.

ILEA (1985). *Profiling in Secondary Schools.* ILEA.

Mansell, J. (1979). *A Basis for Choice.* FEU.

Rowntree, D. (1977). *Assessing Students: How Shall We Know Them?* Harper and Row.

SEAC (1990). *A Guide to Assessment.* Packs ABC.

Hohmann, M., Banet, B. and Weikart, D. (1979). *Young Children in Action.* High Scope.

'Interviews are always nerve-racking.'

CHAPTER 7

The Feedback Loop

Continuing professional development

From 1990 all previous arrangements for the planning and funding of inservice education and training will be changed. This removes once and for all the 'grace and favour' attitude that some authorities have towards the professional development of teachers. It will bring it into line with commerce and industry, and tie it into proper systems for identifying training needs.

The core of the recommendations from the Advisory Council for the Supply and Education of Teachers (ACSET) is for a 'more systematic approach . . . at school and LEA level, which would seek to match training both to the career needs of the teachers and to the desired curricular changes in schools'. HMI also point out in *Quality in Schools* that:

> no less important will be a continual and collective commitment on the part of teachers themselves to such development, and a readiness to see their career as one of continuing growth. The foundations for this view of professional life must be established during initial training. *Students should become accustomed to question, to debate, to analyse, to argue from evidence, and to examine their own habitual assumptions. They should accept that self-evaluation, and appraisal by others, are essential to the conduct of professional life.*

The italics are mine: the indications are clearly preparation for the introduction of teacher appraisal. The Secretary of State for Education has promised guidelines on appraisal, which he sees as essential support for teachers. What is equally essential to such a scheme is Training, Implementation, Management, and Evaluation; in other words TIME. J. E. Jack in 'Appraisal in Schools' makes this point. HMI see the growth of teaching ability as dependent upon the:

extent and depth to which [students] can assess the learning of pupils, relate it to their own teaching performances, and then plan the next activities accordingly. Consequently, the ability to undertake self-evaluation successfully is essential if the students are to continue to develop their professional skills during their teaching careers.

The message is clear. Start with self-appraisal, and then appraisal from other professionals will not only be more comfortable, but you will be in a strong position to contribute to it yourself, and to that of others.

Teacher appraisal

If the principles of the last chapter are accepted, then those proposed in this chapter will seem to be a logical extension. Those principles were that assessment is essential to see if progress has been made; without careful records this is not possible; the process of assessment should be on-going, cumulative and constructive, and all those concerned should be involved in, and contribute to, the records.

What, then, is the main aim of teacher appraisal? According to the National Appraisal Project it is about improving the quality of teaching and learning, by supporting and meeting identified needs in the professional development of teachers. This is very similar, in fact, to accepted practice in business and industry where it has long been seen as the mark of a good employer to promote the careers of their employees. There, no-one would resist the idea of their annual review, although they might view it with some apprehension, for it is often the time for discussion of salary rises and promotion prospects.

Why is there this long standing resistance to appraisal in the teaching profession? Perhaps what George Porter describes as 'that extreme form of fear – ignorance' is at the core. Many older teachers have not had the benefits of the techniques now used on your training courses of being observed in action and deriving insight from the feedback. Until very recently, except in nursery and infant classes, what went on behind the closed classroom door was entirely the teacher's concern, and another adult entered at their peril. It was a singular feature of British schools that the teacher had absolute autonomy on the methods of delivery and most other matters in their own private domain. It was 'the kingdom of the classroom', where they, and they alone, ruled supreme. What went on in the next door classroom was no concern of theirs, and so, many excellent, but idiosyncratic, teachers developed their teaching styles. It was a wasteful system, for much good practice developed, but blossomed unseen and the seed was not spread. Less gifted teachers struggled unsupported and uninspired.

The student teacher and new teachers in their first post should have no such misplaced fears about intrusion in their class. Indeed you will not only be used to being observed whilst teaching, you will have done some observation yourself, both of experienced teachers and fellow students. If your course is a good one you will also have encountered a variety of micro-teaching techniques, and possibly had opportunities for team teaching.

Some interesting points have emerged from the six pilot schemes of the Appraisal Project. Once teachers accept that the scheme is not threatening; not about probing weaknesses, but about developing professional skills, and that they have a stake in its design, they have become enthusiastic. In Newcastle, for instance, some of the perceived benefits noted by headteachers have been:

● Improved relationships within school
● Development and better understanding of working as a team
● Working together for mutually agreed objectives and facilitating agreement about them
● Time and opportunity for teachers to consider what they are doing
● Teachers feeling valued; heightened self-esteem; motivation
● Opportunity to share experiences, for example, classroom visits
● Identification of good practice – with beneficial effect on provision and presentation in classrooms
● Opportunity to liaise with other schools – *in phase and cross phase*

One formative system of appraisal devised by teachers and described by F. Kelly in ' "Teacher Appraisal Working Together" in Perspective' is now operational in pilot schools in Newcastle. Its components form an on-going supportive system. The appraisal cycle begins each time with a meeting between the appraiser, and the person being appraised.

The intention of this model is to provide a framework for each school to develop its own system which accords with its philosophy and particular circumstances. The end result should be a whole school policy from which staff development needs are met in a coherent and efficient way.

There are many other models developing, but from all the present

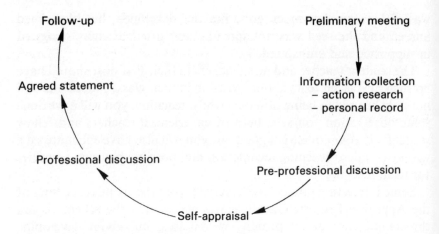

schemes the most frequently requested form of appraisal from teachers has been for class observation. This is hardly surprising given that you will spend over 90% of your working time in class.

The above model lacks any form of external moderation, surely an essential ingredient in the opinion of some (Hancock '90). One of the proposals made by Hargreaves for reform in teacher education is for the first year of teaching to be considered as an extension of initial training. Were this to be so, then some form of involvement by an external moderator would be necessary and beneficial. This might also be seen as a safeguard for new teachers who find themselves in less-than-perfect schools!

The school's aim in teacher appraisal is to develop a coherent pattern of staff development which improves the quality of the delivery of the curriculum. Where do your aims fit into this process?

Your professional aim is to develop a teaching personality which is flexible and stimulating. It will assume that you have an attitude that learning and growing are life-long occupations which do not cease when you leave school, or gain qualified status. This, of course, will fundamentally affect the way you teach and pass on your enthusiasms, as well as the way you plan your career.

Relationships

In previous chapters the importance of developing good relationships with pupils has been discussed. But it must not be forgotten that efforts have to be made to establish good working relationships with colleagues as well. Obviously you are not going to get on with everyone on the staff equally well; some you will like and feel more in sympathy with than others. But remember you are all there to do the same job, so a *modus vivendi* has to be found. A sense of humour is invaluable of course, and the phrase 'I'm sensitive; you're touchy' is salutary! Learn to tolerate the foibles of others.

Self-appraisal

A good start to this process is through the notes or journals you keep whilst on teaching practice. The comments made by students verify this. They range from being tactfully reminded about what was 'suitable' garb to analyses of how a particular lesson went; what elements succeeded, and *why*. Equally valuable is an honest analysis of failures and how you propose to alter your practice to remedy them. Do not be afraid of uncertainty, for it is through a sensitive (though not 'touchy') response that you develop the potential for adaptation of approach – a crucial quality in any teacher.

Be a SWOT; work to strengths; identify weaknesses;

Reports

During and after initial training you will be the subject of a number of reports which should be shared with you. There will be those on teaching practice, and one or more during your probationary period. Usually they will be divided into professional areas such as 'Preparation of lessons'; 'appropriate use of materials and resources'; 'Presentation skills'; 'class relationships'; 'management of time'; 'appropriate level for age and ability of children in class'; 'up-to-date and meaningful records', and so on.

A very useful exercise for you in attempting self-appraisal is to draw up a list of areas for consideration that is pertinent to your situation, and to write your own report on yourself. It doesn't have to be shared with anyone, so be totally honest . . . and professional. By that I mean writing objectively and fairly in professional terms about your attributes and talents.

Do a *SWOT* – that is make a list of your *Strengths*, your *Weaknesses*, the *Opportunities* that you can see in your present situation, and the *Threats* from potential problems or challenges to be overcome. The exercise serves two main purposes.

(1) For you to identify your own strengths and weaknesses, and plan action accordingly.

(2) Use it to compare the reports written by other professionals on you. Is there a significant gap in their and your perception of you?

This is an extremely difficult skill to acquire, but will serve you well in providing you with an ability to contribute in a proper fashion to the appraisal of colleagues at a later date.

Following the popular development of Profiles of Achievement in schools, Hargreaves suggests a similar method of on-going assessment should be used for students in teacher education. This, he claims, would provide continuous, precise feedback on specific areas of competence. He would go further and replace the present simple pass/fail system with a Record of Achievement that the student could take away and use. It would give a clear picture of a wide range of attainment, progress, strengths and weaknesses over the first year of training. He goes further and suggests that the first year of teaching be regarded as an extension of initial training and that appraisal continues along these lines, thus leading naturally into continuing appraisal and professional development.

Job descriptions

A good job description gives you not only a clear picture of the school and department or class for the vacancy, but a detailed list of duties and responsibilities. It often consists of three parts.

(1) The job specification: this should tell you the purpose of the job (ie class teacher for a specific group; subject specialist for certain year groups, and so on), and the main activities and responsibilities of the post.

(2) The selection criteria: this should describe the key skills, experience and knowledge which are considered to be necessary in this post. Shortlisting will be done to these criteria, so make sure you have read them carefully, and covered them in your application form. They will include qualifications; experience; knowledge bases (ie curriculum and teaching methods, managing pupils, pastoral care), and skills (ie organisational ability, written and oral communication, leadership and ability to work with people).

(3) Background information. This section should tell you to whom you will be responsible, and possibly, with whom you will work; the teaching load; the physical conditions (ie own classroom, split

site) and general information about the school, its community and its place in it, curriculum and other developments being undertaken and other current issues facing the school.

The foregoing describes the ideal job description. You may, however, get one that is considerably less clear and full than this one. Try to sort out the information given into the above three categories. It will help to clear your own thinking about whether you want to apply, and then how best to fill in the application. It will also highlight the gaps in information which you may want filled either before, or at interview.

Job applications

Initial training courses vary in the amount of attention given to this very important step in one's career. The next sections cover the essential points to remember.

References

You will always be asked for references. At college your tutors will be willing to provide these. Later when you have left for some time and are seeking a new post you will want referees again. Good manners and common sense dictate that you should *always* get the consent of all referees before quoting their names. For one thing they will all be busy people with a number of other similar requests at the same time. If they are conscientious they will want to do their best for you and will therefore need information from you as to the nature of the job for which you are applying, and an update on your career.

The application form

In completing an application form always give your career to date (or *Curriculum Vitae*) starting with the most recent jobs or courses, and working backwards. If you have had previous jobs list them in this fashion. If you have had part-time or holiday jobs include them also. It helps to fill out the picture of the sort of person you are. Similarly, in the section for further studies or other interests, include the societies and groups you have belonged to as well as sports and other interests you may currently, or in the past have, pursued; Youth clubs, helping with children's camps, Brownies, Scouts. These all help to display a rounded personality showing interests in, and awareness of, the world outside education.

Legibility is paramount. It is astonishing how many teachers send an illegible or misspelled application form, seriously expecting to gain employment from it! There is little excuse these days for not being able to gain access to someone's typewriter or word processor, if your handwriting is nothing to boast about. (Indeed, if this is the case you'd better do something about it, as a good cursive hand is one of the requirements of the national curriculum!)

Usually you are offered the opportunity, either somewhere on the form, or elsewhere, to write a short account of yourself and why you feel you should be given the job. This is, in some ways, the most crucial part of your application and you should give it a great deal of thought and effort to produce a concise account. Providing you have the necessary qualifications for the job, the thing that gets you short-listed is the interest you can generate in the jaded reader in about 200 words. Possibly she or he has had to plough through a dozen or more similar applications. This does not mean indulging in flights of fancy or purple prose, but an enthusiastic approach to the perceived challenge of the job, and what you can offer or bring to it, will certainly receive serious attention. After that, you can do no more than post it and wait!

Interviews

On arrival it is usual for the senior teacher to meet you and put you at your ease. They may arrange for you to be taken round the school while waiting your turn, but ideally you should have had the opportunity to visit beforehand. If you get the chance, talk to the children and try to get a general feel for the place to assess whether or not you might be happy there.

Interviews are always nerve wracking. They do not get any less so with age and experience. Recognise the symptoms in yourself and learn to cope with them. Be comforted by the fact that everyone else being interviewed is suffering, even if it doesn't show. You will, of course, have thought carefully about how you will dress. Extremes of style, whether formal or informal, are out. Clean, neat, tidy, business-like (with tie if male) should be your aim. Avoid fussiness. The secret of confidence on such occasions is to wear something which *you* know looks right, and in which *you* feel happy and comfortable, so that you can forget all about how you look, and concentrate on the business in hand.

A detailed reading of the job description is essential. Try to get as much information as possible on both the job and the school beforehand. Think of all the questions you are likely to be asked, about you, your strengths and weaknesses, and what contribution you can expect to make to the job and the school as a whole. Anticipate searching questions on your understanding of the teaching methods and ages and abilities of the children. Finally, when you think you have been let off the hook, and no more questions are asked, you will be asked if you have any questions yourself. This often 'throws' candidates, for at a good interview most of your questions may already have been answered. Don't hesitate to say so. It shows that you had anticipated them, and are paying them a compliment which never goes amiss.

If you can, have two or three questions prepared beforehand. For instance, after all the professional issues have been dealt with you may want to ask where you can get help and information on accommodation. Important as this is in your mind, do not bring it up before the end of the interview. Other issues such as availability of courses and opportunities for further training, especially probationer induction and support, should be raised now if they have not already been dealt with. Finally, thank the interviewing panel briefly for your interview.

In some schools it is the practice to give a 'de-briefing' after the interview. This is designed to give feedback on how well you did; how you presented yourself, and answered the questions; on which points you did well, and where, perhaps, you should give some thought for the next time.

All that remains now is for me, along with your friends to wish you luck!

References

ACSET (1988). *Report of Advisory Council for Supply and Education of Teachers.*
Hancock, R. (1990). *Teacher Appraisal and Self Evaluation.* Blackwell.
Hargreaves, D. (1989). 'PGCE Assessment fails the Test' *Times Educational Supplement.*
HMI (1987). *Quality in Schools.* An HMI Survey 83–85. DES.
Jack, J. E. (1990). 'Appraisal in Schools' *Head Teachers Review.*
Kelly, F. (1989). ' "Teacher Appraisal. Working Together" in Perspective'. NAIEA.

'Life support systems.'

CHAPTER 8

Life Support Systems

This chapter is about what should be available to you as help during your teaching practice and at other times in school during your training period. It is also about the kinds of continuing support you should expect in your first post.

'Every school needs to have an overall plan for students' says Michael Marland in *The Craft of the Classroom*. Unfortunately not all schools do. The aims of this plan are twofold: to coordinate the work and links between the school and training institutions, and to provide clear guidelines to all staff on their roles regarding student teachers, probationers and the induction of new staff. Part of this policy should include the designation of a senior member of staff with responsibility for arranging the visits, placements and work of students. In a large school they will liaise with heads of departments, decide the proportions of time to be spent observing and teaching, monitor your progress, give you regular and frequent feedback and counselling, and generally keep an eye on your welfare so that you feel you have one person to whom you can go for help and support. They should also ensure that you have the opportunity to visit all departments and units in the school, for such an opportunity seems to be rare once you are established. It is essential if you are to get any sort of a picture of the school as an entity. It is surprising the number of experienced teachers holding management positions in large schools, who have no idea of the workings of some other departments in their own schools. Additionally your mentor should ensure that although you may not take on pastoral and general supervisory duties during teaching practice, (and on the whole you should not be so required), you should have the opportunity to observe these roles in action.

The probationer

It is hard to predict the needs of new and probationary teachers as their situations, expectations and levels of expertise are so very individual. Heading the list must be an understanding of the functioning of their LEA, and the systems and procedures that operate in the school, and the timing of them. From the start you will need to know the procedures regarding registers, accident and incident reports; what the main events in the school calendar are, and whether you are expected to have prepared anything for them. These will include departmental meetings, assemblies, festivals and so on.

Other areas of difficulty commonly quoted are discipline problems either with the class or with individual children. Dealing with groups with widely spread abilities is difficult, not only for probationers, but also for many experienced teachers, as are organisational problems, the use of audio-visual aids and other technical equipment, and keeping records.

At the personal level difficulties are frequently experienced over health, tiredness, 'the blues', and, increasingly, accommodation and travelling.

Secondary teachers in their first year(s) are often worried about their subject areas, particularly in finding appropriate teaching levels and the pacing of work. They may also find that they need to know more about developmental levels of their pupils and their language development. With increasing emphasis on all teachers contributing across the curriculum in personal and social education, many may feel inadequately equipped for this task.

A number of schools are now making appointments for teachers with responsibility for staff development, and it is to them you will need to go. They should arrange regular meetings with you to explain their dual roles of adviser and assessor in relation to your probationary period. I am sure they will invite you to contact them at any time, and you may feel diffident or shy about 'bothering' a busy senior member of staff with what you think they may regard as your trivial problem. Don't, because they are there for that purpose – at least for part of their time in school.

If at all possible they should arrange an extended visit to the school in the term before you take up your appointment. This will give you a clearer picture and time to reflect and prepare. Part of your induction programme will be in school and part, together with other probationers from the area, at the local teachers' centre for professional development.

The sessions with your school tutor should cover such matters as meeting other members of staff, general information about the school, the classroom procedures and methods. They should also deal with record keeping and assessment, and parents' evenings. There should also be professional help in lesson planning and preparation (for the reality and longer term planning necessary is bound to be different from teaching practice, however well you did). This should link with observation and feedback. If the staffing situation allows it you should have the opportunities not only to visit other classes in school for observation, but also to visit other schools, departments or units in other schools in the authority. A visit to a school in a different phase to yours is sure to be an enlightening experience, especially if it is to be a younger phase or a special school. It should help you to identify a little better some of the difficulties which your own pupils may be experiencing with you.

Some schools 'pair' a teacher in their second year with a probationer, in the way that some schools allocate older children to provide friendly initial support to newcomers. This works well in schools where it is possible.

LEA support and induction schemes

In the past several LEAs have operated quite comprehensive induction schemes for their probationers, arranging for them to be released from their schools for a half-day a week to attend special courses run at the teachers centre by a range of experienced teachers, advisers and inspectors. Whether or not these continue under the new funding arrangements remains to be seen, although there is now a statutory requirement for authorities to provide for the professional development of all teachers.

Professional bodies, and unions

Education is political. It always was, and always will be. Plato said education is concerned with how society produces its leaders and policy makers. Today this is even more true, with the declared need for the country to have a workforce of 'knowledge workers' (Drucker, 1989; Stonier, 1979), capable of responding to the fast developments in the Information Technology age. Rajan (1990) argues that schools and employers need to coordinate and broaden their education and training roles if the present weaknesses are to be overcome. This criticism and concern which comes from all sections of society is an issue that must be addressed by all teachers in the next decade. You are in the front line.

Recently, previously inconceivable action by teachers in the form of strikes and withholding of labour has brought about deep divisions between teachers, LEAs and Government, as well as in the profession itself, some of which are slow to heal. Fundamental ethical decisions are called into question; some must be made personally.

Most of you will have received information from the major unions explaining their function and what they offer. In summary, their functions are:

(1) To represent members in negotiating both nationally and locally, teachers' pay and conditions of service.
(2) To provide professional help and legal advice to members.
(3) To publish journals, pamphlets, information sheets and hand-books on relevant topics.
(4) Many offer personal services such as discounts on car insurance, goods and holidays, and personal property cover whilst at school.

Most unions offer student membership.

Membership of a union is a matter of personal choice. It is not compulsory.

Professional Associations exist, usually for specialist areas of teaching. For instance many English teachers belong to the National Association of Teachers of English; many teachers in special schools and classes belong to the National Council for Special Education, or if in mainstream schools, the National Association for Remedial Education, although there are plans for these to amalgamate under a national umbrella of all groups concerned with special educational needs. The benefits of membership of these professional bodies are to keep you up to date with developments within the field, and to put you in touch, usually at local level, with fellow workers. For the new teacher these are benefits worth considering. It should be noted in passing that subscriptions are allowable against income tax!

The law as it affects teachers

First appointment

Once you are appointed to a post in school you should be sent two documents from the authority. First, a contract stating the terms and conditions of employment, which you should receive within thirteen weeks of appointment and which you are required to sign. Under the new regulations these will state the hours you work and may be specific about the duties you will undertake; secondly, a copy of the administrative 'Memorandum 1/83', Education (Teachers) Regulations 1982, (Schedule 6) from the DES, or its successor, or the Authority's Statement of Practice. This DES memorandum is a set of guidelines to local authorities relating to the law on the ways probationary teachers should be appointed and helped to develop.

All employers are now bound by the Race Relations Act 1976, and Sex Discrimination Act 1975, and many authorities describe themselves as Equal Opportunity Employers. Some are more assiduous than others in their application, and it is still notable that although there are more women than men teachers in senior posts and headships men outnumber women by a considerable margin.

If you are taking up a post in an independent school there is no statutory requirement for a probationary period. If, however, you subsequently move to a maintained school, you will have to complete probation satisfactorily, which may, if you have been teaching for a considerable period of time, be waived or shortened.

During your probationary period two reports a year must be written on your conduct and performance. These should be discussed first with you, and a copy given to you. The sorts of support that you have a right to expect during this period are dealt with elsewhere in this chapter. If they are not forthcoming, or you feel they are unfair or inadequate, you have recourse to help outside the school, such as your local adviser or inspector who has responsibility for probationers. The important thing is not to let difficulties go unchecked. Wherever possible probationers should be given a teaching load rather less onerous than one they can expect later, and there should be opportunities to work with, and watch, successful colleagues.

The prospect of dismissal is not likely to be uppermost in the mind of a new teacher embarking on a long career. Nevertheless it should be borne in mind that procedures exist to dismiss unsatisfactory teachers and in really serious cases of misconduct to 'strike them off'. The DES has an official 'List 99' containing the names and reference numbers of teachers found to be guilty of the following offences.

(1) Sexual offences and violence involving children or young people.
(2) Other serious kinds of violence.
(3) The misappropriation of school monies.

124

(4) False claims of a gravely deceptive nature as to qualifications.
(5) Repeated misconduct or multiple convictions unless of a minor kind.

Teachers on this list may not be employed by local authorities.

Conduct and procedures in school

In general, laws relating to health and safety at work are the same as in commerce and industry. Every school is required to have a health and safety representative, and for the most part the rules are predictably common sense. Make sure you are familiar with the ones pertaining to your school so that you avoid any obvious pitfalls.

A guiding principle to remember is that you are regarded in law as 'in loco parentis'; that is a surrogate parent whilst children are in your care. Generally speaking, the authority and court are likely to support you if you acted as any reasonable parent would have done in the circumstances. Laws affecting schools and teachers are designed to ensure the uninterrupted education of children and their safety whilst at school or undertaking educational experiences organised by the school, whether in school time or not. It is therefore sensible to find out what guidelines the authority issue, and what rules particular to your school are in force. Enthusiastic young teachers do not transgress knowingly and most mistakes arise from a misplaced desire to help either a child or a colleague. Unfortunately ignorance of the law is never an excuse, so check if you are at all uncertain as to the legitimacy of a course of action. Whilst not wishing to dampen enthusiasm for giving pupils interesting experiences, or wanting to help individual pupils (such as a lift in your car), it is wise to check if your insurance covers you, or what accepted practice is in the particular instance. This probably sounds cold and inhuman and against all that has been said about building good personal relationships, but prudence should dictate action rather than the heart or temper!

Outings and school journeys can be of immense educational and social value, affording both pupils and teachers time to get to know each other as 'human beans' on neutral grounds. This can be one of the most rewarding (if exhausting) aspects of teaching. But every teacher's nightmare is of the headlines in the press if anything should go wrong and an accident happens. Accidents *do* happen, but are less likely to, and you are less likely to be held to blame, if every precaution was taken beforehand. Schools often require parents to sign indemnity forms covering specific trips and outings in which the teacher in charge is named. As a rule this should not be a probationer, although of course you will welcome chances to be an assistant. Teachers should never take a group of children out alone in case one child has to return to school; there should be a man and woman if the group is mixed sex; the ratio of adults to children should not exceed 1:10, less if the children are very young; and any medical condition that may give rise to problems should be made known by the parents to the teachers. Asthma, epilepsy and heart troubles, for instance, are conditions which may require emergency or prompt treatment. This is especially important if the trip is abroad and there is an emergency which gives no time to contact the parents for consent to treatment. Special vigilance is also needed for such children in swimming pools and the gym.

Another area of worry for students and new teachers is that of punishment. Corporal punishment in any form is now illegal in line with all European countries. The safest rule to set yourself is 'never touch', even in jest or friendliness. This has to be interpreted with common sense in the case of nursery age and very young children, many of whom still need physical reassurance from a friendly adult. The limits of punishment are summarised by Partington as:

(1) The punishment should be given 'in good faith' and be reasonable in the circumstances. (That is, not excessively harsh or vindictive).

(2) The person giving the punishment should bear in mind factors affecting the child.

(3) The punishment should be such that the parent of the child might expect it to receive if it did wrong.

(4) The punishment should be such as is usual in the school.

Punishing a whole class is a quick way to destroy any relationship with them. Imagine if you were in a stream of cars, some of which were exceeding the speed limit, and the police booked them all for speeding!

In matters such as other studies in school the law is sometimes obscure, as it only pronounces when laws are called into question, with the result that there are many grey areas. Supervision before and after school and during breaks, and cover for colleagues have been the subjects of much dispute in the recent past. Check the accepted practices in your school and authority. What is not in dispute, however, is the 'ten minute' rule, by which the law requires teachers to be in school and ready to receive pupils ten minutes before the official start time, and to remain for ten minutes after the finish to see them off the premises. In practice many headteachers require their teachers to be there earlier, or to stay later. Also many teachers prefer, or find it necessary, to stay on to do their marking and preparation work.

An excellent and readable book *Law and the New Teacher* by John Partington covers most of the above in greater depth, giving case studies to illustrate points. Unfortunately it is now out of date in the areas covered by the new legislation in the Education Reform Act 1988, and other allied acts on copyright and the Children's Act 1990. It is out of print, but still worth getting from the library, for its general advice and commonsense approach to legal matters.

A final comment on two unlikely, but tricky, areas that carry potential hazards. What should you do if a pupil gives you information in confidence which involves serious breaches of the law, such as possession or dealing in drugs, or, increasingly, sexual abuse within the family? You may, understandably, feel that it would be a betrayal of trust that has taken you considerable time to build with that particular child, to divulge this information to others. On the other hand, not to do so places you in a position of complicity in the illegal act. Difficult and painful as it will be, this has to be explained to the child, together with the reassurance that no direct blame will be attached to them, or the source of information made known, if that is at all possible. It is important that the child is helped to understand that their best interests are your priority.

With the increasing requirements to keep careful records, you may well decide to keep your own private notebook in which you jot down observations and comments about lessons, colleagues and children. It is worth keeping at the back of one's mind, that, in the unlikely event of a major dispute in the school, all such records and 'private' notebooks may be required to be produced in court. In short, do not commit to paper anything you would not be prepared to stand by in a court of law.

Resources

For your further professional development you should have access to an educational library, although in more rural areas this may be some distance away. Local libraries will always try to obtain books for you, either from county sources or through the national library service.

As mentioned earlier, professional journals are one of the best ways of keeping abreast of developments in your field. Often these are available in the staffroom, and you should certainly find them in your local teachers' centre. Large databases such as NERIS are increasingly available and useful for gaining specific information on resources and equipment.

School magazines or newsletters provide useful background information and help you to gain a 'feel' for the school.

Personal and social life

Workaholics are boring and do not make good teachers. You may feel that the pressures of work assignments and preparation for teaching practice leave you no time for a social life at all. Clearly these commitments must be met and receive priority, but you should also make time and space for yourself – to do whatever it is that you enjoy and is relaxing. As a probationer you may feel particularly isolated, if, for instance, you are in an unfamiliar or large city where you know few people. Teachers' centres may be the answer, as most have a social element to them, often having evening social clubs through which you are likely to make friendly contacts, and maybe gain help over accommodation, and other problems. If your authority runs induction courses for probationers you will have the opportunity to meet other likewise benighted souls to have a mutual moan, and exchange views and local information. You might also get round to discussing broader professional issues, feeding your own intellect and 'recharging the batteries'.

Many authorities are expanding the role of their teachers centres to become Teacher Education Centres or Professional Development Centres to accommodate the new requirements for INSET. They should provide ongoing opportunities for your professional development and counselling, as well as more informal support.

Morale

Morale amongst teachers as a whole has been very low since it was felt that the profession has been under attack from all sectors of the population – government, industry and commerce, parents, even a member of the royal family! Add to that the need to digest all the new legislation and it is not surprising that exhaustion and cynicism are rife. The swings and roundabouts of teacher supply and demand add to the confusion. In the 1970s there were more jobs than teachers; serious cutbacks in training places in the 1980s and a surplus of teachers, led to many excellent students qualifying with no hope of a job. Once again, there is a teacher shortage. It would seem a crazy situation due to an inability to use demographic evidence to regulate provision for the right age groups!

On teaching practice

You are in a catch 22 position in many ways, for, as you will be well aware, you are not a 'real' teacher, yet you wish to make a contribution to the learning of 'your' pupils, which you hope will be recognised and evaluated constructively. Often pupils will also be unclear of your status and be uncertain how to treat you. 'Give 'im a chance' a tough 15-year-old commanded her class mates when a diffident student was struggling to make himself heard!

You will want realistic critical feedback from the class teacher in order to improve and hone performance. Being ignored, destructive criticism, or uncritical fulsome praise are not helpful.

Take comfort from the fact that it is an almost universal experience on teaching practice for students to worry about the seemingly unbridgeable gulf between what you have been lead by your tutors to believe is educationally desirable and possible, and the practices you find yourself observing and having to adopt. This is a real moral dilemma for many students encountering for the first time the tired cynicism of some teachers, together with the harsh realities of the day-to-day functioning of the average school. It is very difficult not to be affected by these attitudes, and sometimes it may seem that anything takes priority over what you thought teaching was all about. There is currently a weariness in teachers battered by mountains of paper which cannot be ignored but which must be digested and responded to. This often requires changes in practice which may have become ossified. Do not mock the aged and afflicted, for it is extremely painful to move an arthritic joint in unaccustomed directions...

Timetables. You will have been allocated classes and a timetable about which you have not been consulted, and which, at worst, has been constructed out of expediency for the school, rather than for your learning experiences. In a school cramped for space you may well have no base from which to organise your work.

It is to be hoped that you will not encounter more than a few of the difficulties described here, but it is as well to 'be prepared'.

A further worry will almost certainly be what to do about individual difficult children. There ought to be some relief system available, a operating even a well devised and defined referral system is energy sapping and time consuming, and is not what teaching practice should be about.

In matters of dress you may think you are sartorially acceptable, but on your preliminary visit, cast a sharp eye on what other younger members of staff are wearing and take your cue from them. You may well have strong feelings about what is, or is not, appropriate for you and your personality, but for the moment, suppress them in the cause of the greater good.

In your first post

It may be of comfort to know that research shows that attitudes on teaching fluctuate markedly in the first years of teaching. Many studies, including that of Wragg in 'Review of Research in Teacher Education', show a manic-depressive 'W' shaped graph, with high aspirations at the beginning of the course, low in TP, high during the next institution based phase, low in the probationary year, and so on.

In your first post be realistic and do not try to change the world, or even the entire school system. Many 'problems' are school created, but to change them needs a whole school policy, which has to be developed by consensus. Tackle what is feasible, realisable and within your remit. Beware the crafty headteacher who tries to exploit your fresh enthusiasm, and offers you the 'opportunity' to take on extra curricular clubs and activities out of school hours, (if you don't feel madly keen). Yes, all in good time, but, remember to pace yourself. Do not exhaust yourself, for exhaustion leads to susceptibility to colds, and then all the ills that children are heir to will be your lot in that first year.

The realisation that, unlike teaching practice, when you had the support of your tutor or class teacher, the sole responsibility for the class is now yours can be terrifying.

Go gently with yourself to begin with: don't try to use *all* your best ideas at once. Experienced teachers pace themselves and husband their energies through the day, the week, the term and so on. It is an essential knack for survival.

Finale

The HMI survey of teacher training found that in the best of lessons observed:

'the organisation and management of the class were well conceived and were carried out with precision, good humour and common sense, with the result that the student established subtle but firm class control. The student had clearly learned a good deal about group observation, managing equipment and resources, involvement in pupils' practical work, and the appropriate management of time available.'

That seems as good a recipe for success as any.

As a final fillip, remember that most schools and many teachers welcome students, and feel that the benefits that accrue to teaching practice are mutual. They say that they enjoy the freshness and enthusiasm of young teachers. It keeps experienced teachers on their toes, stops them from becoming stale, and often provides them with new ideas, for the mark of a 'good' teacher is someone who never stops being a learner.

References

Drucker, P. F. (1989). *The New Realities*. Heinemann.
Marland, M. (1976). *The Craft of the Classroom*. Heinemann.
Partington, J. (1984). *Law and the New Teacher*. Holt.
Prowse, M. (1989). 'The Need to Stay the Course', *Financial Times*.
Rajan, A. (1990). *1992: A Zero Sum Game*. Ind. Soc.
Stonier, T. (1979). *Address to NCSE Bradford*.
Wragg, (1982). *Review of Research in Teacher Education*. NFER/Nelson
Race Relations Act 1976.
Sex Discrimination Act 1975.
Education Reform Act 1988.
Children's Act.1990.

On a personal note

I hope your introduction to teaching is happier and more supported than mine was and that this little book will go some way to providing initial support. It may help you to avoid some of the crasser pitfalls. Perhaps because they are so obvious, experienced teachers forget they have to be avoided, and assume that you already know these things.

I vividly remember my first day's teaching. I was greeted by the headteacher who took me to my (empty) classroom, devoid of cheer and equipment, and handed me my timetable. She then departed for a driving lesson, and I was not invited to speak with her for the rest of the year. I saw her only at occasional assemblies and when driving round the school grounds with her instructor. (I wonder if she ever passed?) By way of support the deputy told me my predecessor had failed her probation because she could not keep order, and when entering my noisy classroom one day, gave me my only instruction in class control by yelling 'Be Quiet' and then dropping her voice to an authoritative whisper. 'It always works', she remarked, 'shouting at them is useless.'

She was right. On at least one occasion when things got too out of hand, I retreated to my stock cupboard and was sick. 'Why on earth did she stay?', I hear you ask, and, 'Why regale us with her murky past?' For two reasons.

First, I hope the support structures for new and probationary teachers are now substantially better. (If they are not – ask someone at your local Teachers' Centre why.)

Secondly, to reassure those of you who are less than confident that it *is* possible to improve your teaching skills, and that many of them come only with time and experience. Don't believe otherwise. I was into my second year when I suddenly became aware that, not only was I not dreading each day, but that I was positively looking forward to working with the children, passing on my own enthusiasms, and planning new courses of work for them.

Finally, my especial thanks must go to Ellis James-Robertson, 'Bob', who, as Senior Teacher and Head of Science in a large secondary school honed his performance skills over many years and kept his sense of humour. His apt and lively cartoons are splendid leaven in my bread!

Glossary of educational acronyms

ACSET	Advisory Council for the Supply and Education of Teachers
AT	Attainment Target
AWMC	Association of Workers for Maladjusted Children
BM	Behaviour Modification
BTEC	Business and Technician Education Council
CAMPUS 2000	The educational network from British Telecom and *The Times* – includes DES database
CATE	Council for Awards in Teacher Education
CPVE	Certificate of Pre-vocational Education
DES	Department of Education and Science
ERA	Education Reform Act 1988
ESG	Education Support Grant
HMI	Her Majesty's Inspectorate
ILEA	Inner London Education Authority
IQ	Intelligence Quotient
JMI	Junior and Mixed Infants
LEA	Local Education Authority
LEATG	Local Education Authority Training Grant
NARE	National Association for Remedial Education
NATE	National Association of Teachers of English
NCC	National Curriculum Council
NCSE	National Council for Special Education
NFER	National Foundation for Educational Research
RSA	Royal Society of Arts
SAT	Standard Assessment Task

SEAC   School Examination and Assessment Council
SEN   Special Educational Needs
TGAT   Task Group on Assessment and Testing
TVEI   Technical and Vocational Education Initiative

Key Stages – the 4 stages during the period of compulsory education to which the National Curriculum will apply.

Education Act, 1981 – The Act relating to the assessment and provision of 'statements of need' for children deemed to have special educational needs.

Statemented Child – a child who has been assessed under Section 1 (2) of the 1981 Education Act, and is the subject of a statement of special need if s/he has a learning difficulty which requires special provision to meet those needs.

Further reading

For Early Years

> Hohmann, M. (1979). *Young Children in Action*. High Scope
> Banet, B. and Weikart, D.
> (for programmes of learning.)

For Primary:

> ILEA (1986). *The Junior School Project*. ILEA.

For Secondary:

(1) Marland, M. (1976). *The Craft of the Classroom 'a survival guide to classroom management in the Secondary School'*. Heinemann.
(2) ILEA (1984). *Improving Secondary Schools*. ILEA
    (principles of good practice.)
(3) Wildlake, P. (1987) *How to Reach the Hard to Teach* OU
    (practical advice.)

On Assessment and Records:

> Hull, J., Powell, E. and Cooper, L. (1989). *Assessment and Record Keeping for SEN in Mainstream Schools*. Hull Associates
> (a 2 part pack including record forms, obtainable from Jean Hull Associates, Honywood House, Lenham, Kent, ME17 2QB.

On Disabilities in School:

> Male, J. and Thompson, C. (1985). *The Educational Implications of Disability*. RADAR
> (A must for every staffroom concerned for children with SEN.)

On Special Educational Needs:

(1) NCC (1989). *Curriculum for All*. NCC
   (implementation of NC)
(2) Brennan, W. (1985). *Curriculum for Special Needs*. OU

On Behaviour Management:

(1) HMI (1987). *Education observed 5. Good Behaviour and Discipline in Schools*. DES
   (Very succinct account of general principles.)
(2) Westmacott, E. and Cameron, R. J. (1981). *Behaviour Can Change*. Globe.
   (An easily readable account of realistic BM in the classroom.)
(3) Wolfendale, S., Bryans, T. (1989). *Managing Behaviour*. NARE.
   (A brief practical framework for schools.)

Useful General Backgrounds:

(1) Clegg, A. and Megson, B. (1968). *Children in Distress*. Penguin Edition Special.
   (A classic 'oldie' but still very relevant.)
(2) Webb, L. (1967) *Children with Special Needs in the Infant School*. Penguin.
   (Another classic: practical common sense.)
(3) Rutter, M., Maughan, B., Mortimore, P. and Ouston, J. (1979). *Fifteen Thousand Hours*. Open Books.
   (Classic research on what actually happens. A study of 'broader patterns of life in schools and kinds of environment for learning which they present to their pupils'.)

The excellent DES *Teacher Education Project* published by Macmillan has a series of Focus books edited by T. Kerry on: class management; effective questioning; mixed ability in the early years of secondary school; handling classroom groups; teaching bright pupils explanations and explaining.

Index

accent 30
accidents 124
Aids/HIV positive 59
arousal 63
Arrival and dismissal procedures 26
aspects of achievement 95, 104
assessment methods 95, 96
'assessment through teaching'
  model 91
assessment
  continuous 96
  criteria for 100
  diagnostic/prescriptive 94
  observation 98
  purpose and function 92, 93
  self 99
asthma 57, 125
Aston Index 92
attainment 41, 94
attention 62, 63
authority guidelines 124

behaviour
  A,B,C of 80
  checklists 77
  disturbed 78
  disturbing 79
  consequences 79
  modification techniques 79, 82
  contracts 83
Bettleheim 68
Bloom 39

Brown 69
Bruner 66
Bullock report 45, 67
bullying 86

cerebral palsy 56
checklists 6, 28, 60, 61, 77, 81, 97
child development 36, 69, 81
Childrens Act 1990
chronic medical conditions 58
class control 40, 41
classroom observation techniques 12
classroom arrangements 22, 24
'clumsy child' 56, 69
concentration 38
conditions affecting central nervous
  system 56
CPVE 102
criterion referenced tests 97
cystic fibrosis 51

dance 67
dealing with interruptions 27
designated teacher for SEN 53
diabetes 57
dialect 30, 45
discipline 75, 86, 87
Downs syndrome 57
drama 67
Drucker 121
drugs 126
dyslexia 56

Education Act 1981 70, 134
effective schools 6, 75, 86
Elton Report 86
employers 102
epilepsy 56, 125
Equal Opportunities Employer 123
equal opportunities 46, 69
expectations 24, 25, 68, 92
expressive arts 67, 68

feed forward 94
feedback 94
'fuzzies' 81

games 64
good teachers – features of 8, 9
grammar 30
Gronlund 96
Gunzberg 101

Hancock 112
Hargreaves 6, 8, 112, 114
hearing impairment 21, 58
Hegarty and Lucas 96
hidden curriculum 25, 37, 87
High Scope 66, 99
homeostasis 21, 27, 28
Hull 69, 91, 94, 99, 103

ILEA The Child at School 76
induction programme 120, 121
intelligence 51, 52
interviews 116, 117

Jack 111
job descriptions 114
job applications 115

Kelly 111
Koestler 44

language
    across the curriculum 45
    delay 67

development 45, 47
impairment 58
in the secondary school 46
jargon 45
register 46
Laslett 84
laws affecting teachers 122, 126
learning environment — criteria for
    28
learning difficulties
    diagnostic screening 62
    definition 70
    identification 60, 61
learning
    theory 37
    sequences 62
London Record of Achievement
    101
Mager 81
Mansell Report 'Basis for Choice'
    101
Marland 26, 119
Maslow 21
meeting individual needs 66
memory 66
Meredith 79
micro teaching 31
morale 127, 128, 129
motivation 38, 78, 79
multi-cultural 47
multi-ethnic 47
muscular dystrophy 57
muscular and skeletal abnormalities
    57
music 67, 68, 84

negotiation 83, 87
Nolan 69
nursery rhymes 65

objective tests 97
Overstreet 51

'pairing' 121

Partington 126
pedagogy 2
peer tutoring 100
performance 2, 81
personal study skills 17, 18
personal and social life 127
personal appearance 16, 17, 116, 129
Pestalozzi 72
physical environment 21
Physical education 69
praise 87
presentation skills 43, 44
Priority Problem List 81
probationary period and reports 113, 123
probationers 24, 120
professional associations 122
professional development 10, 35, 110
Professional Development Centres 120, 127
profiles 92, 94, 101, 102
Prowse 130
psychological environment 24
punishment 85, 87, 125

Race Relations Act 1976 123
racial harassment 86
raising standards 29
Rajan 121
record keeping 94, 103, 126
records of achievement 92, 114
references 115
rehearsal 65
Reid 42
reinforcers 83
relationships 113
report writing 104
responsibility for learning 66, 87
Rowntree 18, 91

S.E.N. chap 4, 99, 102, 103

safety and incident reporting procedures 124
sanctions 85
school created difficulties 60, 87
school visiting 12, 71
school procedures 15, 125
school journeys 124
science 70
seating arrangements 26
self esteem 65, 68, 92
self evaluation 31, 110, 113
Sex Discrimination Act 1975 123
sexual abuse 28, 84
'sitting next to Nellie' 14
skill 79
spelling 29
spina bifida 57
staff handbook 16
standard English 29
standardised tests 52, 95
Standards in Schools
statemented child 71, 103, 134
Steiner 68
Stones 36
Stonier 121
Stott 21, 28, 35, 61, 63, 78, 79, 96
'SWOT' 113

task analysis 65
teacher appraisal 3, 110, 111
Teacher Education Centres 129
teacher training - HMI report 10, 53
teacher tutor 1, 6, 14
teachers with responsibility for staff development 119, 120
teaching strategies 62, 69
teaching practice 13, 22, 42, 128
teaching methods 39
  groups 41
  mini-teaching 42
  mixed ability 42
  whole class 40
TVEI 102

unions 122
Upton 87

visual impairment 21, 22, 59
voice 31

Warnock report 53, 67
Weikart 66
Westmacott and Cameron 81, 82
Wiltshire 39, 69
Wragg 129